How to Buy Bank-Owned Properties for Pennies on the Dollar

A Guide to REO Investing in Today's Market

JEFF ADAMS

WILEY

John Wiley & Sons, Inc.

**To the unwavering patience and tireless
support of my wife Kristina...
And in honor of my twin daughters Tatum and Finley**

Published by John Wiley & Sons, Inc., Hoboken, New Jersey.
Published simultaneously in Canada.

For general information on our other products and services or for technical support, please contact our
Customer Care Department within the United States at (800) 762-2974, outside the United States at
(317) 572-3993 or fax (317) 572-4002.

Wiley publishes in a variety of print and electronic formats and by print-on-demand. Some material
included with standard print versions of this book may not be included in e-books or in print-on-
demand. If this book refers to media such as a CD or DVD that is not included in the version you
purchased, you may download this material at http://booksupport.wiley.com. For more information
about Wiley products, visit www.wiley.com.

Library of Congress Cataloging-in-Publication Data:

Adams, Jeff, 1964-
  How to buy bank-owned properties for pennies on the dollar: a guide to REO
investing in today's market / Jeff Adams.
    p. cm.
  Includes index.
  ISBN 978-1-118-01834-7 (cloth); ISBN 978-1-118-13356-9 (ebk);
  ISBN 978-1-118-13354-5 (ebk);   ISBN 978-1-118-13353-8 (ebk)
  1. Real estate investment. 2. Foreclosure. I. Title.
  HD1382.5.A336 2011
  332.63´24—dc23

                                        2011017546

Printed in the United States of America.

10 9 8 7 6 5 4 3 2 1

CONTENTS

Part I

THE INVESTING OPPORTUNITY THAT WON'T COME AGAIN IN YOUR LIFETIME

Chapter 1

THE PERFECT NIGHTMARE FOR BANKERS—A DREAM COME TRUE FOR INVESTORS

Be greedy when others are fearful—and . . . fearful when others are greedy.

—Warren Buffett, legendary investor and chairman and CEO of Berkshire Hathaway, Inc.

In the wake of the Great Recession, and the bursting of the real estate bubble, American banks have been repossessing homes at the rate of more than 1 million per year. This is terrible news for the banking industry, but it represents an amazing opportunity for investors and homeowners who aren't afraid to buy when others are running from real estate. Never before in history have the markets been so overwhelmed with so many properties, so few buyers, and such low interest rates. Rock-bottom prices like this probably won't happen again in our lifetime.

Welcome to the reality of today's real estate market. In 2010 alone, a record 2.9 million properties faced foreclosure filings—that's 1 in every 45 homes across the United States. It was the fifth straight year those numbers climbed, according to RealtyTrac (www.realtytrac. com), an industry organization that tracks foreclosures. Not all foreclosure filings end up as home repossessions, but banks and lenders did repossess more than 918,000 homes in 2009 and more than 1 million in 2010, according to RealtyTrac.

Causes of the foreclosure debacle range across the board—from homeowner job loss to divorce, medical issues, death of a spouse, overall economic conditions, and much more. These problems were made systematically worse by the bursting of the real estate bubble and plummeting property values. But the root of the problem is that many Americans simply bought homes beyond their means—often with adjustable rate loans or interest-only loans. As property values collapsed and those mortgages adjusted or corrected, overextended homeowners found themselves upside down on their mortgages—owing more on their properties than the properties were worth—and unable to refinance or afford the payments.

People's homes ended up in foreclosure, and a big chunk of those foreclosures didn't sell at auction and thus became real estate owned (REO) properties—that is, properties owned by the bank. It's the perfect storm that creates high profit potential for investors who understand how and where to find the information to turn this tragedy into a viable business opportunity and help America's real estate market get back on its feet.

The massive foreclosure wave isn't over yet. In 2010, nearly 10.6 percent of all residential real estate loans were delinquent, according to the Federal Reserve (www.federalreserve.gov/releases/chargeoff/delallnsa.htm). That's more than 1 of every 10 properties. RealtyTrac predicted that lenders would repossess another 1.2 million homes in 2011.

NUMBER OF REOS IN THE UNITED STATES	
2006:	268,532
2007:	404,849
2008:	861,664
2009:	918,376
2010:	1,050,500
Total:	3,503,921

Source: RealtyTrac (www.realtytrac.com).

To say it's a buyer's market is a vast understatement. If you are an investor who knows how to capitalize and profit, this is your time and your opportunity to cash in—full-time or part-time—to create a secure financial future for yourself and your loved ones.

WHAT IS BANK-OWNED REAL ESTATE?

When a homeowner misses three or more mortgage payments (the number varies by state), the property goes into default and typically the foreclosure process begins. However, not all homes that lapse into foreclosure end up foreclosed or bank-owned. A homeowner in default, for example, could make up the missed payments or sell the property to an investor or another buyer. But in many cases foreclosure does occur. If no one then buys the property at auction, it ends up as an REO, a bank-owned property. Today hundreds of thousands of homes worth millions of dollars have become REOs. Because banks aren't in the primary business of owning real estate—instead, they lend money, issue credit cards, and provide other financial services—the REOs tie up banks' valuable lending capital and wreak havoc on their balance sheets. That's why banks are willing to unload the properties at a fraction of their real worth—for pennies on the dollar.

"This is the greatest time in history to buy (a house)," real estate genius Donald Trump said in an interview with Sean Hannity. "Even if you don't have money, the banks will make you a deal." (www. realestatewebprofits.com/trump)

Pennies on the Dollar

Just how much are banks willing to deal? Discounts can be as low as 50 cents on the dollar and even lower in some cases. That's because many banks are struggling to get out from under bulging portfolios of repossessed properties they don't want.

Nonproducing Assets

Each REO is an empty house that's considered a nonproducing asset—it weighs down a bank's balance sheet, costs the bank money to maintain, and can have a detrimental effect on the bank's ability to loan money. For each nonproducing asset, banks are required to have offsetting liabilities that show up as loan loss reserves on their balance sheets. (Banks use complicated formulas to determine the amount of loan loss reserves required.) In the banking industry, capital (or net worth) is the difference between the bank's total assets and its total liabilities. An increase in liabilities—REOs—squeezes or shrinks the bank's capital reserves. With a smaller capital reserve, a bank may face higher costs to borrow money from the Federal Reserve Bank. That's the money a bank typically lends out.

If the bank has a big enough loan loss reserve, the Fed may prohibit it entirely from making further loans until it reduces its loan loss reserve. That can be accomplished by getting rid of—selling off— its REO properties.

So the banks want to sell, and if your approach is right, they'll do so usually quickly and cleanly. Today you can find hundreds of millions of dollars in real estate owned by banks—and not just in California, Nevada, Texas, and Florida (states with the highest foreclosure rates). It's happening all across America. Never before have home prices been this low, combined with super-low interest rates. Homes in the United States are on sale!

Real Deals

In 2010, I went shopping for bank-owned real estate and picked up several properties *on sale* in Southern California, each for less than $162,000, and at 60 to 65 percent of their market value. The after-repair value (ARV) in today's market of each of the homes ranges from $200,000 to $250,000. I bought a property on West Rosewood Street in Rialto, California, for about $122,000, rehabbed it, then sold it for $155,000. My profit on the quick deal: $15,000.

A SAMPLE OF RECENT DEALS

What kinds of deals are available out there today? Here's a sample of a few California properties I purchased in 2010. The after-repair value (ARV) of each of the houses ranges from $200,000 to $250,000 based on 2011's market prices.

1010 Moffatt Street, Rialto: **$153,845.49**
137 S. Terrace Road, San Bernardino: **$139,061.23**
587 W. Winchester Drive, Rialto: **$134,081.97**
951 E. Home Street, Rialto: **$161,562.72**
352 W. Rosewood Street, Rialto: **$121,570.09**

The Fear Factor

Most people are afraid of what's happening in the housing markets and the economy, so they sit on the sidelines of the housing market.

As an investor, I recommend buying as many of these on-sale properties as possible at huge discounts today, flipping (selling) some, and holding others as rentals. No matter what's happening now, property values will eventually rise. I actually think they're going to skyrocket.

"Be greedy when others are fearful—and . . . fearful when others are greedy," says Warren Buffett, president and CEO of Berkshire Hathaway, Inc., and one of the richest men in the world. He has a point. Now is the time to be greedy!

HOW I GOT STARTED

I know what it's like to be fearful and struggling, and desperate to find a way to financial freedom. I was there, and then REO investing changed my life. I am living the life of my dreams today, and it's the result of what I have learned about how to invest in REOs.

As an REO investor, I've been involved in hundreds of transactions, and all while investing part-time. That's right. I'm a firefighter by profession. Fifteen years ago, like millions of other Americans, I was working hard but buried in debt and on the verge of bankruptcy. I was struggling to get by in a stuttering economy. My dreams of providing for my family were way bigger than my pitiful bank account. I loved being a fireman, but I wasn't earning much money. I made only $40,000 a year. At one point I was so broke, I was using my Master-Card to pay off my Visa, my Visa to pay off my American Express, and my American Express to pay off my MasterCard. I tried all different ways to find success but failed miserably. I kept thinking that if I worked harder I would get ahead, but it wasn't happening. I even tried a bunch of "get-rich" dead ends.

Then a friend who was a house painter told me about a real estate investor he worked for who had a property in San Bernardino, California, that he wanted to sell at a wholesale price. I'll never forget that first REO deal—at 6747 Sepulveda Avenue. My friend told me the house probably was worth around $75,000 rehabbed, but the investor was willing to sell it for $42,000. At this point I was ready to file bank-ruptcy, so I was willing to try anything. I looked at the house, and while still in front of it, checked with three real estate agents about the property's after-repair value. Each said it was worth $75,000 to $80,000, so I contacted the investor. He told me he had the property under con-tract for $38,000, and that he would assign the deal to me for $4,000 cash. He already had lined up 100 percent financing from a hard-money lender he used.

A hard-money lender is willing to put up cash for a deal at a sig-nificantly higher rate of interest than conventional lenders—gener-ally 3 to 5 points higher—plus various fees. Using these lenders can make sense, especially if you're just starting out, because they typi-cally will lend you 60 to 70 percent of a property's ARV and don't require you to jump through hoops the way a conventional lender will. That means it's not about your credit rating; it's about the prop-erty's value. Using a hard-money lender may mean spending an extra $5,000 to $7,000 on a deal, but your loan will be funded quickly and simply.

I was broke and desperate, so I took out two $2,000 cash advances on credit cards to provide the $4,000 cash and financed the rest through the real estate investor's hard-money lender. The price for the house was $42,000 plus fees that included title, escrow, closing costs, and fire insurance. The house needed work, and of course I had absolutely no idea how to rehab a house. I did it, though, with the help of "Home Depot University." I sold the house three months later and made $12,000 on the deal. Today, whenever I walk by that house I bend over and kiss the sidewalk in front of it. That humble little abode is what set me on the path to financial freedom. See Figure 1.1.

I used that initial $12,000 profit to stave off my creditors and then went about developing my part-time REO investing career. Since that initial real estate investor introduced me to hard-money lend-ers, I was able to do deals even though I was broke. Hard money doesn't come cheap, but it's simply part of the cost of a deal, and the profits more than make up for it. As I became more successful, I was

My First REO Deal

Figure 1.1 6747 Sepulveda Avenue, San Bernardino, California. This was my first house.

able to transition from using hard-money lenders to using private investors, who were able to provide me cash and flexibility based on my track record rather than a specific property's value. I used credit card cash advances to pay for the materials I used to fix up the houses on those first deals. I would work to rehab the properties on weekends and on my days off from my still full-time job as a fireman. I made the commitment because I had decided this was the business I wanted to be in.

Back then there were no how-to manuals with tips and tools of the trade. I learned the right way to do deals by trial and error. I quickly found out that buying and selling REOs was the best way to financial freedom because it meant dealing directly with banks and not dealing with unmotivated tire kickers—homeowners who aren't sure they want to sell, who have emotional involvement with the properties, and so on.

SAVING YOUR FINANCIAL LIFE

As a fireman, I also was a hazardous-materials specialist and emergency medical technician (EMT). In my job I saved the physical lives of hundreds of people and their pets. My new mission is to help save people's financial lives. What I'm about to share with you can breathe new life into your finances. My system will save you plenty of headaches. Remember, I've been there. I had to learn all this.

REO deals can go wrong in many ways, but I am going to show you what you need to know to avoid the traps. This book explains how to find the best deals, get the best financing without using your own money, and then quickly either sell the property or rent it out. How would you like an extra $10,000 or $20,000 from just one deal? Buying and selling REOs is a plausible and practical way to dramatically increase your financial wealth today and your comfort level for the future. You can do this.

When Californian Scott Cheramie tried REO investing my way, he closed on his first deal within a week and then flipped the property for a $32,000 profit.

Teresa R. Martin, an attorney in New York, bought an REO triplex in her market, also without any money of her own, and then opted to hold it as a rental property with a cash flow of more than $1,000 a month.

DOES THE JEFF ADAMS APPROACH TO REO INVESTING WORK?

Here's a sample of what some of my students have to say about my approach to buying and selling real estate:
"Using these strategies, I put $125,554.51 in my own pocket. . . . I can't thank you enough."
— Cory Harrington, San Antonio, Texas
"I highly recommend his [Jeff Adams's] program to all investors who are looking to get into REO investing and become highly successful."
— Teresa R. Martin, Esq., New York, New York

"Within one week of enrolling in your program, I was able to close on my first REO deal. I was able to resell it for a profit of $32,000. . . . I think your program is great, and I could not have closed on these deals without it."

— Scott Cheramie, California

"The last deal I did, I made a profit of over $32,000 using the strategies that are in your system. I can't say enough good things about the . . . system and the amount of profit it has brought into my company."

— Dale Steinman, Chanute, Kansas

AVOIDING THE MISTAKES

Many people set out to get into the real estate investing market with grandiose ideas to conquer it, but the market ends up conquering them because they don't know what they're doing. They get the wrong kind of guidance or none at all, they don't follow through, and they end up strapped for cash and out of luck. For example, many real estate gurus urge their students to buy every rental property possible. It's the take-care-of-your-cash-flow-needs-tomorrow philosophy. But they neglect to account for the importance of accounting for your cash-flow needs today. That's what almost happened to me. I tried buying rental properties. But my tenants were less than ideal, and they ended up trashing the properties. I was putting in twice as much cash as I was taking out, and I was getting further and further behind financially.

I had to learn everything myself. I didn't have the benefit of others' experience and insight. That's why I decided to create my own step-by-step approach and get it down in a book. In the following pages, you'll learn about the tools you need, with step-by-step instructions on how to use them. You'll learn how to find the best REO deals in your market, find buyers for those properties, access private lenders and cash, close quickly, and flip those properties for quick cash or turn them into ready streams of income as rental properties.

REALISTIC COMMITMENT

"Yeah, right," you're thinking. "That's what they all say."

Often when we hear a persuasive motivator we get really excited about an idea or approach to getting ahead financially; we have the enthusiasm and desire to do something, and sometimes we are even willing to shell out cash up front. Then that initial fire in the gut is tempered by the reality of all the work and time required simply to break even, let alone be successful. The enthusiasm for embarking on the path to financial security gets lost somewhere in our everyday survival.

That's why I've designed the approach in this book to require as little as 10 to 12 hours a week. With the right focus, direction, and drive, almost anyone can realize real financial gains buying and selling REOs. I'll show you what it takes to present yourself as a strong buyer and seal the deal. You'll also learn about the different exit strategies available, with checklists to follow along the way.

This system can help virtually anyone—whether you're a beginner or a seasoned professional, whether you're looking for full-time employment or a part-time supplement to your income, whether you have cash on hand or not. You can learn to be real-estate-wise, to understand market realities, to know how and where to find the money, and to create an REO buying and selling system that works for you.

Chapter 2

WHY REO INVESTING SAVES TIME, HASSLE, AND MONEY COMPARED WITH TRADITIONAL PREFORECLOSURE AND SHORT SALE INVESTING

I like REOs because they are quick.
    —**Alex Galitsky, Florida Realtor and real estate investor**

U ntil now, most real estate investing systems have urged their fol-
    lowers to buy preforeclosures or short sales as the ticket to riches.
With a preforeclosure, the homeowner is in default on the mortgage
but the lender may not have begun the foreclosure process; in a short
sale, a lender is asked to accept less for the property than the amount
owed on the mortgage. Yes, such deals still can be made—and the
profits still are there—but today neither approach is as consistent,
direct, or easy as REO investing.

As a firefighter and hazardous-materials specialist battling some of
the most dangerous fires in California, I quickly learned the importance of assessing a situation, setting a goal, and using the safest, most
direct route to accomplish that goal. I learned to pay attention to the
situation and the surroundings, and then act accordingly. I've made a
lot of money doing preforeclosure and short sale deals. But those
approaches were right for yesterday's economic environment. Market
forces and economics have changed, and so has the best and most efficient way to capitalize on them. You don't have to spend all that time
and energy getting to the deal anymore. REOs are what work best
today. Remember at the height of the real estate bubble when it seemed
as if you needed to win the lottery to pick up a property? Then came
the collapse, and the market was suddenly flooded with properties.
Times change, and so must investment strategies.

THE TIME FACTOR

It's about time—your time. Investing in short sales and preforeclosures
takes too much of your time. There can several reasons for this:

- It's often tough to track down owners.
- If you do find the owners, they could be very difficult to deal with.
- Titles to the properties can be clouded with multiple liens.

- As an investor on these deals, you can spend months on a potential transaction that doesn't materialize.

Of course, banks won't accept every REO offer you make. But with REO buying, no matter your exit strategy—whether you decide to immediately sell (flip) the property, hold it and remodel it to resell at retail, or hold it and rent it—you'll expend less time and energy because you're working directly with banks on properties with clear titles, and without the stress and delays of working with homeowners in default.

2010 HOME SALES AT A GLANCE

(% of total sales)

Damaged REOs: **13.7%**
Move-In-Ready REOs: **15.6%**
Nondistressed (normal retail sales): **53.6%**
Short Sales: **17.1%**

Source: Campbell/Inside Mortgage Finance HousingPulse Monthly Survey (www.campbellsurveys.com).

Let's look more closely at foreclosure and the various acquisition processes.

FORECLOSURE BASICS

Foreclosure is a process that extinguishes all rights, title, and interest of the owners of a property in order to sell the property to satisfy a lien against it. That's why it often takes so long. Laws and procedures that govern mortgage default and foreclosure vary by state, but there are two basic approaches to foreclosure in the United States. About half the states use the "power of sale" approach, and the other half use "judicial foreclosure." The former involves a "power of sale proceeding," which is dictated by a deed of trust and the trustee (usually an attorney or title company). The trustee informs the property owner that the debt has not been paid. The lender then specifies a due date for payment of the debt. If the payment isn't processed within the specified due date, the lender issues a stronger demand for payment. If the debt is still not met, the property is sold at auction. The period of time between the demand for payment and the resultant property auction varies by state. In the other approach—judicial foreclosure—the lender files a lawsuit in court against the homeowner in default with the intent to reclaim the property.

Wherever you opt to invest, it's important to know and understand the state and local rules and regulations governing foreclosure. General information on various state foreclosure laws is available at Realty-Trac (www.realtytrac.com/foreclosure-laws/), but always be sure to contact a government entity in the area, too, to verify foreclosure rules and regulations.

Basically, however, when potential investors talk about buying properties in the various stages of foreclosure, they refer to one of the following three situations:

1. **Preforeclosure.** Dealing with a property owner in default on a mortgage and/or a property involved in the foreclosure process; this includes short sales.
2. **Purchasing a property at auction.** An auction, sheriff sale, or trust deed sale, when the mortgage holder forecloses on the property and forces the sale of the property, ideally to recoup some or all of the debt.
3. **REO.** After the property has been foreclosed, fails to sell at auction, and its ownership reverts back to the bank/lender.

STEPS TO FORECLOSURE

- **Nonpayment:** Typically lenders allow occasional late payments on mortgages for a small fee and a notation on the borrower's credit report. However, after the third missed payment, a lender generally sends a past-due notification.

- **Default:** If payments continue to slide, the note becomes a default and legal action is initiated. The lender issues a demand letter asking for full and immediate resolution of the debt or else foreclosure action will ensue.
- *Lis pendens* **("suit pending"):** This is a formal notice of default that is filed against the property.
- **Complaint:** This formally lists the events leading up to the foreclosure on the property, and includes the history of the mortgage debt.
- **Judgment:** Final judgment occurs after a set period of time as determined by state law. At this point, the homeowner can rectify the situation by paying the mortgage current plus all fees and legal costs to date.
- **Redemption period:** The time allotted to the mortgagor to reclaim his/her property after it has been sold at an auction. Not all states have a redemption period.

Problems with Preforeclosure and Short Sale Investing

As we discussed, a homeowner is in default when he or she misses a certain number of mortgage payments—more than 1 of every 10 mortgages across the United States is delinquent today. Technically, a mortgage goes into foreclosure after the third missed payment. But financial institutions don't always issue formal default notices so quickly, especially in today's market.

Why not? First, banks face a huge backlog of foreclosed properties. Second, hundreds of thousands of homeowners today find themselves upside down on their mortgages—the amount of the mortgage exceeds the current value of the property (negative equity)—so even if a bank repossesses a property, it never recoups its investment. As of year-end 2010, more than 11 million mortgages—23.1 percent of all residential properties with mortgages—were in negative equity, according to

CoreLogic, providers of consumer, financial, and property information and analytics and services to businesses and governments (www.corelogic.com/About-Us/News/New-CoreLogic-Data-Shows-23-Percent-of-Borrowers-Underwater-with-$750-Billion-Dollars-of-Negative-Equity.aspx).

One way homeowners try to get out from under this upside-down debt is through a *short sale*. In a short sale, the homeowner must prove financial hardship; usually must have a ready, qualified buyer; and must ask the bank/lender to take less for the property than is owed on the mortgage. In essence, the borrower wants to "short" the bank on the payback and wants the bank to forgive the difference. (There still can be tax consequences, however, so it's important for the homeowner to check with a tax adviser.) The process involves an avalanche of paperwork, and there's no guarantee a lender will accept a short sale, which can and does generally take months to finalize. The process can be further complicated by second and third mortgage holders and liens that often show up against the property at the last minute. Just because a property owner has a guaranteed buyer does not mean a short sale is a done deal, either.

Chris McLaughlin is a Lakeland, Florida-based real estate broker, investor, and attorney who owns four Keller Williams Realty offices in the Tampa area (www.mclaughlinchris.com). In 2010, his offices—with their total 450 Realtors—oversaw at least 600 short sale completions. But, says McLaughlin, that's out of thousands they tried to complete. "Our success rate is probably around 20 to 25 percent," he adds.

Officially, for every 2.7 offers made on a property, 1 short sale is completed, according to data from Campbell/Inside Mortgage Finance HousingPulse Monthly Survey.

In the meantime, while the homeowner and potential buyer jump through the required hoops and play the waiting game, the property can (and today often does) end up trashed or vandalized—or, worse yet, squatters could move in. A lender, too, might foreclose on a property before a short sale is completed.

Two Colorado real estate investors, Ellyn and Bill (their names have been changed to protect their privacy), opted to purchase a preforeclosure property as a short sale. It was a great house, in great shape, and in a great location—an excellent investment, they agreed. Initially they became interested in the property and a short sale as a way to help out their neighbor, Lou, who had lost his job and recently divorced his wife. The plan was for Ellyn and Bill to buy the property at a discount and turn it into a prime rental, while saving Lou's credit at the same time. Lou said he would move out as soon as the deal was done. The four-bedroom/three-bath split-level home was valued at $353,000. The short sale price was $289,400 (just under 82 percent of the value; in short sales banks typically will take 80 to 82 percent of the after-repair value [ARV] of a property).

Ten months after the process was initiated and after Ellyn, Bill, and Lou had provided reams of paperwork—much of it duplicates—to the bank, the bank finally agreed to the short sale. Ellyn and Bill were thrilled. The property was move-in ready, and already they had ideal tenants, who had agreed to a substantial monthly rent. Everything was going as planned, or so the pair thought. But it turned out that the hassle of completing the short sale with the bank was the easy part of the deal! Getting Lou out of the house was quite another matter.

A full 13 months later—that's 13 additional months of Lou living in the house as a squatter and not paying rent—he finally left. Ellyn and Bill had considered getting the sheriff to evict Lou, but they felt sorry for their onetime friend and opted not to try that route. By the time Lou left, the "ideal" renters were long gone and the house was trashed inside. Lou had allowed the house to deteriorate as a way to decrease its value, so instead of only a few hundred bucks to paint the place, Ellyn and Bill had to spend thousands of dollars to clean up and rehab the property—they even had to replace all the appliances. It took them several more months to find good tenants. "I learned my lesson about short sales—too much hassle—never again!" says Ellyn.

Ellyn and Bill could have considered waiting for the bank to fore-close on the property instead. They then could have either approached the bank to purchase the house as an REO or found an investor—possibly like you—willing to flip the property to them wholesale for a flat finder's fee.

Not every aspect of a short sale is negative. Alex Galitsky, also a Realtor in central Florida (Charles Rutenberg Realty, Orlando, Florida [www.eHouseBuyers.com/]) and a successful real estate investor, points to some advantages of short sales: "You put out a lot of offers, and some will come together and some won't. I like short sales because there is less competition, fewer people willing to wait that long for an answer. Short sales often can come with a tenant (already in the property) and that can mean cash flow from day one."

Nonetheless, Galitsky prefers REOs because they're quick. "With an REO deal, within a week you know the offer is accepted and you're moving forward, or you know that your offer isn't good enough. With a short sale, it can take months to get a response or get a response that your offer isn't any good, or that the bank already has foreclosed."

Let's look more closely at some of what's generally involved in finding and completing a real estate purchase in either a preforeclosure deal or a short sale. (Note: Homeowners often back out of either type of deal at the last minute.)

Preforeclosure

(Length of time start to finish: Can take weeks or even months; no guarantee of completion.)

- Identify properties in default—after a homeowner misses three or more mortgage payments.
- Locate and contact the property's often unresponsive and uncooperative homeowner (expect doors slammed in your face and phones hung up numerous times).
- Convince the homeowner (who often truly does have a hardship story) that your intentions to buy the property at below-market prices are the best option, a win-win situation for both of you.
- Run the numbers and put together the offer.
- Check for clear title; correct any title issues.
- Locate the money to finance the deal.
- Finalize the deal.
- Close the deal.

- Get the property owner out of the home—it's not always easy and sometimes can involve the sheriff.
- Re-key (change the locks on) the property.
- Pick up the pieces—it's not uncommon for the homeowner to vandalize the house inside and/or outside on the way out the door. Some angry homeowners will put cement in the toilets, for example, or destroy or walk off with appliances, among other possible damages and thievery. Think Lou, earlier.
- Repair the house, which even if new can be run-down—homeowners who have defaulted on a loan may not have had the money or incentive to maintain the property.
- Create a marketing strategy to sell or rent the property.
- Follow through.
- Seal the deal.
- Cash your profit check.

Short Sale

(Length of time start to finish: Drags on for months; no guarantee of completion.)

- Identify properties.
- Locate and contact the property's owner (expect doors slammed in your face and phones hung up numerous times). If a house is vacant (owners today often will simply walk away from upside-down mortgages), it can be difficult to locate the property's actual owner.
- Convince the homeowner (hardships or not) that you can help by approaching the lender about a short sale.
- Run the numbers and put together the offer.
- Check for clear title; correct any title issues.
- Provide extensive paperwork to lender, including proof of homeowner's hardship, proof of the dramatic drop in property's value and why it won't regain that value in the near term, and proof of your qualifications to purchase the property.
- Locate the money to finance the deal.

- Wait for bank to say yes or no.
- Complete more paperwork in response to bank inquiries.
- Wait again.
- Complete more paperwork
- Wait again.
- Finalize the deal (or walk away).
- Close the deal.
- Get the property owner out of the home. That's not always easy as Bill and Ellyn, earlier, found out. (Sometimes difficult owners can be lured out with cash in exchange for keys to the property.)
- Change the locks. It's about keeping the old owners out.
- Pick up the pieces—here, too, a now-former homeowner often vandalizes the house inside and/or out on the way out the door.
- Rehab/repair the house, which usually is in disrepair.
- Create a marketing strategy to sell or rent the property.
- Follow through.
- Seal the deal.
- Cash your profit check.

As an investor, would you prefer to go through the headache, emotion, hassle, and time-intensive approaches of preforeclosure or short sale purchases, or go the route of a clear-cut REO deal with no emotions and no headaches? The REO approach is to locate a property, deal directly with the entity (the bank or other lender) that owns the property free and clear, make your offer, and seal the deal. It's really a no-brainer for most investors who value their time. If done right—and in these pages you'll learn how to do it right—your REO purchase can take as little as a few days. Even Realtors Chris McLaughlin and Alex Galitsky, who both know how to make short sale investing work, like the ease of REOs. The bargains are plentiful, too, says Galitsky. For example, in central Florida as of early 2011, REO condos were selling for 25 cents on the dollar, as compared with prices at the height of the boom. That means a condo worth $200,000 at its peak could be purchased for $50,000! At the same time, investors also could pick up townhouses for just 35 cents on the dollar and single-family homes for 50 cents on the dollar (again that's assuming the "dollar" is the price at the peak several years ago).

YOU CAN DO IT, TOO

One easy way for beginners to get started is to work with a buyer's agent. For example, even now Galitsky likes acting as a buyer's agent. He locates the REO deals for a group of investors and takes a smaller profit on each REO deal—perhaps $1,000 to $5,000 per deal—as commission. But he makes up the difference with high volume. "I get a little profit without any risk on my part," he says. "It takes minutes to do the paperwork."

Where do you get the money? You may start out finding and flipping properties to other investors in your market—using their money—and earn a finder's fee or commission. That's what Galitsky does, and it's also a great way to get started in the business. This is your time and your opportunity to capitalize. You can do it coast to coast—California to New York, Florida to Texas, to Minnesota and beyond.

Chapter 3

HOW TO OVERCOME YOUR FEAR, SET GOALS, AND GET STARTED

This is going to be the hardest thing you ever do, but it will be the most rewarding because it creates generational wealth.
    —**Zack Childress, successful real estate investor and Jeff Adams Foreclosure Academy instructor**

Because today's once-in-a-lifetime sale on real estate is so vast, everyone—young and old, beginner or seasoned veteran—is clamoring to buy properties, right? Not exactly. The reason: As human beings, we are prone to inaction, especially when it involves unfamiliar territory or something outside our comfort zone. We may know that something is right and we should do it, but we fail to act.

You can't win, though, if you don't take action. Even lottery jackpot winners had to get up, go out, and buy the ticket first!

Many people realize that the property bargains are out there. They may even talk about that fact as well. But they simply don't get around to doing anything about it. They never play the game. Status quo remains their comfort zone, and fear of the unknown their impenetrable barrier. If you want to get ahead, to get your finances on track and create a secure financial future, you need to do something about it. The universe rewards people who take action. You can't get ahead if you don't do something, if you don't take the first step.

DELAYING TACTICS

Even for those of us who recognize there must and can be a better way, the leap to action isn't always instantaneous. It took me time to get around to taking action. Before I bought my first REO property, I was borrowing off my credit cards to live, while racking up more and more debt until one day I finally decided to do something about it; I decided to take action. I recognized that even though I loved being a fireman and doing what I was doing, it would take a different kind of action on my part if I truly wanted to provide financial security for my family. I would have to veer from my steady-as-she-goes course, step out of my comfort zone, and take action.

Alex Galitsky was born in Belarus and immigrated with his family to the United States in 1991. He didn't speak any English, but he went to school, learned the language, and went on to graduate from college. Then he went straight into corporate America as a software engineer. He was living the American dream, or so he thought. "I was making more money than I ever had before, than my dad ever made," says Galitsky. "Then, I started noticing that the people coming to work were not that well-off. They drove beat-up cars and were struggling financially, even after working in the same place for 30 years. That wasn't right. . . . I started thinking the corporate world maybe wasn't as good as it looked." It was time for action! "That's when I started getting into real estate investing."

Ron Rupert was a salesman at a Cadillac dealership when he decided to take action and get into real estate investing. "I was the smartest poor person you ever met," he says. "I knew everything about sheltering income. I just didn't have any. Education empowered me to go out and find success." Today, he's a successful investment capital expert and real estate investor. "Over the next three to five years, more millionaires will be created than ever before if you know what you're doing," says Rupert.

THE FEAR FACTOR

Fear of the unknown or unfamiliar paralyzes us and facilitates much of our inaction.

> **FEAR (NOUN): THE EMOTION OF BEING AFRAID, APPREHENSIVE AS CAUSED BY THOUGHTS OF DANGER, WHETHER THE THREAT IS REAL OR IMAGINED.**

To be fair, fear is a formidable barrier. That's especially true when it comes to investing in real estate, no matter the current state of the markets, how great the deals and discounts are, or how experienced an investor you are. Fear of real estate investing doesn't have a single cause, either. It's composed of many different fears—a firestorm of fears. Often, we don't even readily recognize the fears in ourselves. Those fears include:

- Fear of investing in real estate because of the recent collapse in property values.
- Fear of a recession or a second Great Depression.
- Fear of a scam, that the good deal is too good to be true.
- Fear that the lack of cash or credit will make it impossible to buy real estate.
- Fear of too much time involved to buy a property from a bank.
- Fear of the unknown.

Nearly everyone who has ever invested in real estate has at some point been afraid in some way. But people who are successful at anything know that fears are countered and controlled by knowledge and understanding. As a potential real estate investor, that's what you must learn. You have to overcome the fears and take action.

THE POWER OF CONVICTION

We discuss step-by-step what it takes to succeed at REO investing later in this book, but briefly consider the following basics when it comes to a few real estate investing fears:

- **Property values that hit bottom will climb again.** Whether home values double-dip and drop again or not, they will eventually climb. They already have in some locales and individual neighborhoods across the country. If you know your market, you'll understand its ups and downs.
- **A market decline, even a recession, means a giant sale.** If you have the cash or know where and how to get it, another market decline is just another opportunity to find bargains that you might never be able to pick up under normal market conditions.

- **Scams are everywhere in anything you do.** The key is to know how to recognize the red flags, and how to avoid the scams altogether.
- **Plenty of investor cash is available if you know where to look and the best ways to get it.** Your profits will more than make up for the cost of that cash.
- **Education is essential.** It can turn the unknown into understandable reality.

Zack Childress, a successful real estate investor who also works with me to help new investors get started, offers an unusual twist on fear of real estate investing: "The number one reason people don't make offers on a property is fear of 'What do I do if they accept the offer?' If it's a deal, your hard-money lenders will be there," adds the self-made entrepreneurial millionaire. "I grew up in a trailer park on food stamps. My dream was to be a successful investor, and it took over my life. I knew it would work, I knew I could make it." And he did.

That kind of conviction helps people overcome their fears. "The average person doesn't get off the couch and is stuck in a rut," adds Childress. "That doesn't mean the average person can't succeed at buying and selling REOs if they have the internal drive to do more. But you aren't an investor until you make an offer."

Brian Holmes agrees wholeheartedly. "My life didn't start out this way," says Holmes, also a real estate investing coach with the Jeff Adams Foreclosure Academy, whose various jobs have ranged from bail recovery agent to stockbroker and now successful real estate wholesaler. "I didn't learn this business the easy way. [But] there is a light at the end of the tunnel. You *can* do what it takes to be successful in this business."

TUNE OUT THE NEGATIVE

Success or failure depends to a large extent on the individual. If we believe we will succeed and do everything in our power to succeed, including getting an education and guidance, our chances for success are far greater than if we doom ourselves to failure. It's that power of positive thinking coupled, of course, with knowledge, direction, and expert guidance.

Real estate investing is no different. In fact, bargains and success stories aside, the negative swirl around real estate investing can be overwhelming, especially in today's struggling economy. Likely most everyone you know or care about (or don't care about) will offer you a horror story of why you can't succeed or a cautionary tale about so-and-so whose life was ruined by real estate investing.

When I first mentioned getting into real estate investing, my family told me they thought I was crazy, and others with whom I shared my dream offered their own horror tales. All this generated what-ifs that threatened my dream.

- What if I can't resell a property after I buy it?
- What if I can't do the repairs?
- What if someone gets hurt on my property and they sue me?
- What if I can't make the mortgage payment?

Of course, it's unlikely that these naysayers have ever invested in real estate themselves.

You must choose to look at REO investing as a way to get financially ahead, and believe that you can do it. If you tune out the negative and approach REO investing with the right guidance, expertise, and attitude, you can succeed, and you likely will. If you don't, the fear will overcome you.

Don't lose sight of the fact that properties, buyers, and sellers are out there if you know how and where to find them and how and when to deal. The nation's population is growing every day. And people, including all those hundreds of thousands who have lost their homes to foreclosure, have to live somewhere.

BEWARE THE BLIND SPOTS

Many people enter the real estate market to conquer it, but the market ends up conquering them because they jumped in and didn't know what they were doing. A real estate deal can go wrong in many ways, but in these pages I'll show you the cautionary flags to look out for and teach you how to avoid the traps.

> People often use negatives to talk themselves out of getting started in REO investing. The reality, however, differs:
>
> - **Negative:** I can't possibly show a bank proof of available funds so that I can make an offer on a property. **Reality:** *Oh, yes you can.*
> - **Negative:** Banks need a large down payment for a deal. **Reality:** *No, they don't, not necessarily in the current market, not even if you're a beginning investor.*
> - **Negative:** I can't assign the contract to someone else, so I'm stuck with the property. **Reality:** *That's just flat wrong. With the right approach, you can assign contracts.*

I'm here to talk not about theory but about what actually happens in the real world. All of the above drawbacks/concerns can be handled with a positive approach that's aboveboard and doable. All the methods are legal and can be done consistently in ways we talk about in Part II.

ANALYZING THE EXCUSES

If fear is the roadblock that keeps someone from buying REOs, excuses are manifestations of those fears. That doesn't make fear any less real, but it does make the excuses easier to analyze, disprove, and disregard. Let's dissect a few of the most common excuses that fuel inaction.

Too Many Offers on REO Properties

> Excuse: Why should I bother to invest in REOs? The field is too crowded already, and too many people are bidding on all the properties. I can't possibly ever win, so why try?

In Chapter 1, you read about the literally millions of properties that have ended up as REOs over the past several years, with another 1.2 million added to the mix in 2011. No matter how anyone crunches those numbers, that's a lot of properties and certainly enough to go around for everyone. Plus, if these REOs are selling so fast, why are banks slashing their prices—selling them for pennies on the dollar? Banks, after all, are trying to recoup some of their losses from foreclosure.

The answer is, the REOs aren't selling that fast. In central Florida, Alex Galitsky points to condos selling for as little as 25 cents on the dollar. That's a 75 percent discount. No retailer or wholesaler of anything offers such discounts unless they're desperately trying to move merchandise. Banks' portfolios of REOs are overflowing with properties. They need to dispose of them, and they will make the deals to do so. Yes, they get offers, but few investors really know what they're doing. Few offers are realistic, clean offers done right—an offer in which an investor supports his price with sound research, provides proof of funds, and has the credibility to follow through. One REO agent friend estimates that 90 percent of the offers are done improperly and are therefore rejected.

Galitsky is also a broker price opinion (BPO) agent. That means banks turn to him to get an opinion on a property's value before they sell their REO properties. Among his pet peeves—and one he encounters frequently—are blind offers on properties. "An investor reads that properties are selling for 'pennies on the dollar,' but he doesn't do his research. He makes an offer on a property at 30 cents on the dollar off the current asking price. The property already is listed (the asking price) at 75 cents on the dollar based on its current value, and already the bank has several offers. That's a quick way to immediately ruin the investor's credibility, and classify him or her as a 'newbie,' " he says.

Smart REO investors outdo the competition by doing their job better. That means better research, quicker responses, building relationships with REO agents, more responsiveness to sellers' agents needs, writing better contracts, continual follow-up, and more.

Now Is the Worst Time to Buy

Excuse: With all the foreclosures out there and properties worth so much less than three or four years ago, this must be the worst time to buy.

Don't let the negative buzz mask the reality. The Big Sale is on. The worst time to buy was in 2006 and 2007, when many home prices were inflated to their peak and beyond. Even in that market, though, if you purchased properties at the height of the bubble in the right place at the right time, and if the price—the discount— was right, and the deal was structured properly, you could have walked away with solid profits. I did, and so did thousands of other investors.

But real estate investing success requires close attention to your market. The adage "location, location, location" means more than where you're buying or selling. What's happening in a specific market, as well as nationally, dictates the exit strategy—whether you buy at wholesale and flip at wholesale, buy at wholesale and flip at retail, or buy and hold as a rental income property.

I Won't Be Able to Sell the Property

Excuse: I'm not buying because it's too hard to sell properties right now.

That's not necessarily the case. Right now interest rates are at near-record lows and the market is primed for first-time homebuyers and investors. If a property isn't selling, it could be in the wrong place or simply not priced right. Another option to flipping a property may be to rethink the exit strategy. It often can make more sense, especially when property values are depressed, to buy and hold a property for its rental income. Currently, I own 11 properties free and clear that provide me more than $200,000 annual income. The fact is that many full- or part-time REO investors look to buy income-producing rental properties to provide them with regular income. The biggest mistake I ever made in REO buying was that I didn't hold on to more properties as rentals. Instead, in the beginning I flipped almost everything.

REO Investing Doesn't Work Here

Excuse: REO investing doesn't work in my area.

Every locale has the potential for investment opportunity. Whether the time is right for that opportunity depends on the current market details and an investor's exit strategy. Research a specific geographic area to determine whether now is the best time to buy and sell or buy and hold in an area, and whether that approach fits with your preferred exit strategy (see Part III). If you ask all the questions you need to ask and get too many negative answers, then move to another potential area and start the process over again.

Eugene Seagriff, for example, targeted Pennsylvania's Lehigh Valley for his real estate investing. Initially he wanted rental income properties, and his research showed the rental market there to be reasonably robust, along with other positive, strong growth indicators, including:

- A growing job market.
- A new casino was under construction.
- A new Wal-Mart.
- Major highways intersecting in the area.
- The fact that the area has warehouse distribution centers.

The bottom line, says Seagriff, is that over the next five years, the area is likely to attract many new jobs; therefore, it's a relatively sound market in which to purchase rental real estate.

KNOW NOTHING/KNOW IT ALL

Excuse: I don't know a thing about REO investing./I know everything and don't need anybody.

Both excuses are equally devastating to a deal. If someone blindly gets into the business without knowing what he or she is doing, that's as bad as someone who thinks he knows the ropes but hasn't a clue. Plenty of real estate investors have tried to do deals and made big mistakes because they didn't know what they were doing, and either they didn't want to seek direction or they didn't know who to ask or where to turn. That's where this book can help.

"The biggest mistake I ever made in real estate investing was when I lost $100,000 on a deal," says Zack Childress. "When I first started, I jumped into rehabbing properties and didn't know what I was doing. I teamed up with a guy who said he knew what he was doing, but he really didn't know, either. We lost the money, lost the home, and he quit. I didn't, because I realized if I had done the deal correctly, I would have made $200,000."

MISTAKES GET IN THE WAY OF REO INVESTING SUCCESS

All of us make mistakes. That's part of the learning curve. It's also an acceptable part of learning any new business. What's essential, though—and what this book will help you do—is to minimize the mistakes. You will learn to anticipate what can go wrong and compensate for it ahead of time. Then, when you do make a mistake, you will recognize how to turn it into a learning experience. That's what Childress did. "I won't make that mistake again," he says. And he hasn't.

Here are a few big REO deal busters. We'll help you understand the details of how to avoid many of them later in the book:

- Would-be investors don't take the right approach to financing. They don't offer banks the proper proof that they have the money to do a deal (proof of funds), and they don't get access to cash before making an offer on an REO property.
- Would-be investors don't work with the right real estate agent or think that they don't need an agent. Often they mistakenly don't bother to develop working relationships with a Realtor and with REO agents. Both are musts for a successful REO investor.
- Would-be investors are confounded by contracts. To write a contract properly, you must understand what you can and cannot do, and what's legal and what is not in your state. Successful REO investors understand the nuances of options like back-to-back closings and why offers with contingencies—dependent on an action, like a property inspection, for example—often complicate and derail deals.

Forget the fears and excuses, concerns and deal breakers that stand in the way of your taking advantage of the fire sale on real estate. It's time for action, so let's get started.

THE FIRST STEP: SET GOALS

Before starting to invest in REOs, it's essential to set goals for your professional investing and personal future. Too often would-be investors overlook the forward-thinking planning and instead jump right in. Without goals and action plans, their grand visions of success evaporate into failure.

Vision is the big picture of what you want over the long haul—financial security, for example. A long-term vision can help motivate you into action and focus what you already know (and recognize some of what you don't know), as well as organize your resources toward achieving your goals. Goals are the near-term initiatives you would like to accomplish—buy one REO property in the next six weeks, for example. They serve as stepping-stones in achieving your vision. Setting well-defined goals also allows you to see growth in areas you once thought impossible, and to measure your success. (Success is a great motivator!)

LOOK FOR ANSWERS

To define your own vision and set your goals, you must ask yourself several questions. Think seriously about each one, and be brutally honest with the answers. Your future depends on it. A few questions to consider:

- What do you really want from your real estate business? What would you like to gain from REO investing?
- What would you like to accomplish over the next 30, 60, or 90 days; the next year; and beyond? Are you looking for properties to flip, to fix up and sell, or to buy and hold for rental income? Or all three options?

- How much time are you willing to invest every month? Do you want to work part-time or full-time?
- Realistically, how much profit would you like to make every month from your deals?
- How much profit do you think is realistic based on the time you have available if, for example, you're a part-time investor? The answer to that question helps determine your exit strategy for any property you buy—what you plan to do with it after it's yours.
- If you're thinking about buying and rehabbing REOs, are you able to do the rehabbing yourself, at least in the beginning? If not, perhaps a different exit strategy is better for your situation, or else the expense of having someone else do the work must be figured into the cost of any deal.

SET YOURSELF UP FOR POSITIVE RESULTS

Once you have defined your vision and set your goals, create a plan of action that includes objectives for each goal.

SAMPLE PLAN OF ACTION

Vision: Retire in five to seven years

Goals to Achieve Vision:

1. Buy and sell two to three REO properties a month for the next five to seven years.
2. Hold one of every four properties (choose one with positive cash flow) as a rental to create monthly income.
3. At the end of five to seven years, sell half of the remaining properties and use the cash to pay off the loans on the remaining properties.

Plan of Action:

1. Review the Multiple Listing Service (MLS) listings every day for new listings, listings that have a revision to list price or price drop, and listings that have been on the market for more than 90 days; and make an offer (60 to 65 cents on the dollar minus repair costs) on every suitable property in your market that fits into your exit strategy.
2. Contact a minimum of five REO agents a week to seek out potential REO properties.
3. Try to attend at least one Real Estate Investor Association meeting a week to network, develop contacts, and seek out deals.
4. Every evening, make a list of follow-up phone calls for the next day.
5. Daily make follow-up (courtesy) phone calls with agents.

It's important to have results-oriented goals as well as performance-oriented ones. For example, setting a goal to earn $10,000 a month within one year is great, but your goals need to define how you will achieve that. To help overcome the overwhelming aspect of starting out in the REO business, set aside specific and regular blocks of time to work, and then work to accomplish one thing at a time. That's especially important if you opt to begin your REO investing career on a part-time basis. Prioritize what has to be accomplished, too.

When I started in the business, I had no one to show me what to do. I struggled, working my full-time job as a fireman and then coming home and doing all it took to flip houses. Fifteen years ago, there weren't as many REOs, either; banks weren't begging for buyers for the properties they did have, and there weren't any how-to manuals — no *Guide to REO Investing*.

I learned the importance of narrowing my focus. Start your REO investing business in a niche. Find a specific geographic area and specific type of property, and concentrate your efforts on that niche. If you diversify too much in the beginning, you'll have trouble getting a deal done. That's what happened to me. At first, I desperately looked at every possible property and every possible transaction to find a deal. All I did was spin around in too many directions. Then I began to focus on specifics—buying, rehabbing, and flipping properties to first-time homebuyers in one geographic area—and I began to be successful. Whether you're buying and flipping wholesale, retail, or buying and holding as rental properties, you must learn to focus your efforts and strategies.

Pay attention to the early planning, follow up and follow through on the execution, tune out the negative, stay focused and committed, and you heighten your chances of REO success. You can do it, and you can do it without prior experience or your own money. Plenty of people have, and they have found and continue to find their financial security in the process.

Chapter 4

OVERVIEW OF THE REO DEAL

REO investing is one of the easiest and fastest ways to achieve lasting financial security for you and your family.

—Jeff Adams

REO investing—whether for beginners or seasoned professionals—doesn't have to be difficult, overwhelming, or scary. If you know up front the steps involved and how to deal with each one, you can come out a winner. Naturally, the road has some bumps along the way—that's a given in this or any other business. If, however, you've done your homework and you've learned about and understand the individual components of the REO investing process, those bumps become minor readjustments along your road to success.

Let's get started on reviewing the road ahead.

THE EIGHT STEPS

No matter what you plan to do with a property after you buy it—that is, whether your exit strategy is to buy and flip, buy and hold, or do something else—REO investing involves eight basic steps with plenty of nuances along the way:

1. Find the money.
2. Research your market.
3. Establish credibility/build your professional team.
4. Find the properties.
5. Evaluate deals and price a property right.
6. Make an offer/negotiate with banks.
7. Apply your exit strategy.
8. Cash your profit check.

It's that simple. Understand the nuances of each of the first seven steps, and the last step—cash your profit check—can become a regular occurrence. We discuss each step in depth in later chapters, but here is a quick rundown.

Find the Money

It's crucial to find the funding for any potential REO deal *before* you search for that deal. Otherwise you could torpedo the deal at the outset. This money-first approach may seem a bit backward. Don't you need a potential deal first? No! Cash up front or proof of funds to do a deal is essential in the REO investing business. Without such guarantees in the form of a proof-of-funds letter, REO agents generally won't waste their time with you, and neither will banks. Your offers immediately will end up in the trash. Banks want to see physical proof that an investor behind an offer has the funds as insurance so they aren't wasting their time considering an offer. Cash in hand also allows you to move quickly when you do locate a deal.

Do your homework and figure out where you can get the cash—think hard-money lenders, for example—and then get proof of access to the cash in the form of a formal proof-of-funds letter. It's possible to fund deals personally—I've used cash advances on my credit cards and hard-money lenders. Eugene Seagriff used cash from an individual retirement account (IRA). We talk more about the options and the importance of the right proof-of-funds letter in Chapter 5.

Research Your Market

Find your niche and stick to it early on. Decide the best location in which to concentrate your efforts, as well as the type of property you want to specialize in and your target buyer or renter. You'll have more success if you target your efforts to a specific area and a specific type of property rather than looking for anything, anywhere. I learned that lesson the hard way: When first trying to invest in real estate, I looked for any property, any size, any condition, and in any area—and ended up with nothing. When I started to focus my energies and efforts, success followed.

In selecting your target market, pay attention to the economic details of the area. For instance, does the area have a solid job market? If you're considering the first-time homebuyer market, does the area have good schools? We discuss these and other economic indicators in Chapter 6.

Establish Credibility/Build Your Professional Team

Credibility in this business, as in any business, is in a large part related to how you present yourself and deliver on what you promise. It's your reputation—personal and professional. As a beginner, pay special attention to how you look and what you do. Present yourself professionally in appearance and action, and you will go a long way toward establishing your credibility as a serious contender in this business. Opt to ignore your professionalism, waffle in your approach to deals, back down or back out of offers, and fail to follow through, and agents will give you the cold shoulder while your offers end up in the trash.

A key to your credibility is making sure the team behind you—all those experts whose support you must have to succeed—is professional, knows what it's doing, and takes pride in doing its job properly. This is your power team and should include a certified public accountant (CPA) with real estate know-how; a banker; a real estate attorney; an appraiser; an investor-friendly title company; a real estate agent (especially for access to the Multiple Listing Service [MLS], which is your window to the deals); a mortgage lender; and a handyman. These people don't have to be your employees, but you do have to develop solid relationships with them so that if you turn to them, they're available and helpful. Check out Chapter 7 for more details.

Find the Properties

With cash in hand, a target market, and a professional team behind you, you're ready to look for the best REO deals. Your local Multiple Listing Service (MLS) is the place to start.

According to the National Association of Realtors (www.realtor.org/law_and_policy/doj/mls_overview):

> An MLS is a private offer of cooperation and compensation by listing brokers to other real estate brokers. . . . MLSs are private databases that are created, maintained and paid for by real estate professionals to help their clients buy and sell property.

In most cases, access to information from MLS listings is provided to the public free-of-charge by participating brokers.

The Realtor on your team can help you get access to the MLS, which lists properties for sale and gives detailed information about those properties.

One of the best ways to continually come out a winner in REO investing is to locate properties as soon as they are listed on the MLS, and then bid on them immediately. Also look for listings that have a revision to list price or price drop, or properties that have been on the market for more than 90 days. If your offer is done right, you substantially increase your chances of getting the deal.

The MLS isn't the only game in town, though; you can bid on properties even before they are listed on the MLS. We talk more about where to go to find the deals in your target market in Chapter 8.

EVALUATE DEALS AND PRICE A PROPERTY RIGHT

Just because an REO sounds great on paper doesn't always mean it's a great deal. Many variables beyond the right price/right location figure into whether a deal is right. A house may be theoretically correctly priced (in line with similar houses sold recently in an area), but closer inspection could reveal that its previous owners trashed the place on the way out. Translation: It will cost a bundle to repair it and bring it up to standards. That means any offer on the REO should take that added repair cost into consideration. Or a house may be priced right in what seems like a good location, except that recent major layoffs in the area could mean the market likely will be flooded with properties and no buyers. The right evaluation of the deal (and researching the economics of a geographic area) would quickly show that the best approach here would be to forget this deal and move to the next.

Similarly, if you're flipping a property but can't find buyers, it could be because the property is priced too high to move. That's a major reason contributing to banks' overflowing portfolios of REOs. Often the banks and lenders priced properties too high at auction so they didn't sell and ended up as REOs. More on auctions in Chapter 10.

Make an Offer/Negotiate with Banks

As you read earlier, you're not an investor until you make an offer. An addendum to that statement might be that you're not an investor until you make a *serious* offer. Too many would-be REO investors send out spamlike standardized offers on properties without any research or any real idea of the value of a property. Banks (and their REO agents) toss those offers, too.

To be successful in this business, an investor must learn the right way to approach and work with banks, and how to word offers to streamline deals, not stymie them. The successful approach is not about tricking the bank or trying to "pull a fast one." The right approach is above-board, honest, and straightforward.

Chapter 12 details the do's and don'ts, along with the tips and tricks of negotiations.

Apply Your Exit Strategy

"Exit strategy" is fancy talk for what you plan to do with the house after you buy it. You're not an investor until you make an offer, and you won't collect any profits until you apply your exit strategy. An exit strategy is like a mini business plan because it should show how, when, and where you intend to make a profit. The profit motive also helps you determine how to price your offer.

If, for example, your exit strategy for a particular REO is to buy it, rehab it, and hold it as a rental property, you'll need to factor related costs into any discounted offer on the property. Likewise, if your exit strategy is to buy an REO and immediately flip it to a wholesaler, that needs to be considered too. (Read more on exit strategies in Chapters 15–17.)

Cash Your Profit Check

After the deal is done, the papers are signed and sealed, and the check is in hand, pat yourself on the back and enjoy the fruits of your labors. Cash that profit check.

REMEMBER THE THREE PS

The three basic principles—the three Ps—of real estate investing are people, properties, and processes. If you keep that in mind and pay attention to the details related to each, you boost your chances for success.

People

Real estate investing is a people-oriented business. Master the art of putting people first, and be sensitive to the needs of the people you deal with, whether bankers, agents, title company clerks, or homeowners. Positive, professional, and upbeat attitudes are contagious. They're also a way to differentiate yourself from the crowd. People will remember you for your professionalism, your personal approach, and your positive attitude.

Properties

Make the most of all the resources available to you to locate, evaluate, and acquire the right properties. That includes reading classified ads in newspapers and online, paying attention to what appear to be abandoned properties in your neighborhood, and much more.

Processes

Successful people focus on the processes required to achieve the desired results. They have learned the right formula or recipe to follow. In the pages of this book, I give you the approaches and the formulas as well as the direction to enable you to develop the right processes for successful REO investing.

Part II

REO DEALS, STEP BY STEP

Chapter 5

WHERE TO GET THE MONEY

*Finding the money comes first and then you're in a strong position
to capitalize on the best REO deals.*

— **Jeff Adams**

M oney comes first in the REO investing business. Banks generally
won't look at, let alone consider, any offers on a property without written proof up front that an investor has the money to follow
through with the deal. If a solid deal on an REO property in your target market comes up, you must be able to move fast. That means you
have no extra time to scramble to find cash.

Before even starting to look for properties, every REO investor must
figure out where the money will come from and then get the proof in
writing that he or she has the money or access to it. That verification is
known as proof of funds.

Don't sweat it, though, if you don't have your own cash. Too many
wanna-be investors do let lack of cash inhibit them, and they sit on
the sidelines instead of taking action. You don't need the bank
account of a Bill Gates or a Warren Buffett to get into this business.
In fact, you don't need *any* of your own cash or credit to get started in
REO investing. There's plenty of OPM—other people's money—if
you know where to look and the right way to get it and use it. The cost
of that cash simply becomes an accepted part of the cost of doing the
deal, and your profits more than make up for any interest charges
accrued.

NO CASH, NO PROBLEM

Today's sputtering economy aside, thousands of potential investors
with millions of dollars are clamoring to find deals in which to
invest their money. Wherever you are in the world, there are people with cash to spare who are willing to put that money to work.
Private real estate investing and private money lending are popular
ways for them to generate solid profits. These people often have

neither the time nor the inclination to look for real estate or other deals themselves, so instead they lend out cash for real estate investments.

Plenty of other creative financing options are available, too. They're legal, aboveboard, and investor-wise. Some banks, mortgage lenders, and mortgage brokers still offer 100 percent financing on certain deals. A mortgage broker generally doesn't have his or her own money to lend but instead will send loan packages to several different sources, hoping one will buy the loan. Also, keep in mind that for long-term purchases such as a buy and hold for rental, it's a good idea to use a bank. (You might make the initial purchase of the property using a hard-money lender or private investor, and then after perhaps six months—after the lender knows you can make the payments—it's worth negotiating a long-term loan with a bank.)

Let's look more closely at some of the various options.

Hard-Money Lenders

A hard-money lender, as discussed in Chapter 1, will put up the cash for a deal based on the value of a property, not the creditworthiness of a borrower. The cost of the cash is higher, generally 3 to 5 points more than a conventional lender plus various fees. With a conventional loan, for example, interest rates could be in the range of 5 to 6 percent, while a hard-money lender might charge 5 points on a loan (i.e., a 5 percent fee on the loan total) with 13–15 percent interest plus $1,500 to $3,000 in various other fees. But these hard-money lenders do quick and clean deals without the hassles of conventional lenders, and as an investor, your profits should more than make up for the higher money costs.

"Small" Cost

Even with the higher rates, though, if an investor buys the property at a big enough discount, the extra points and fees of a hard-money lender are well worth the cost when compared with using a conventional lender. Additionally, a conventional lender requires any potential borrower to jump through hoop after hoop, and there's still no guarantee the lender will grant the loan.

Jordan Cantu, 22, has purchased 10 REOs so far in Southern California for $85,000 to $90,000 each. Each of the properties has an after-repair value (ARV) of around $150,000. That means she bought each property for about 60 to 65 cents on the dollar. Cantu uses private-investor loans at interest rates of 8 to 10 percent on the money. She rents the properties for $1,500 to $1,600 a month, and even with the sizable cost of her financing, she still has a positive cash flow every month. Cantu has big plans for the future, too. She wants to buy a total of 30 to 40 properties; hold them as rentals; and then, when property values appreciate, sell half the properties and use the profits to pay off the other half.

Finding Lenders

For many investors, the idea of approaching private money lenders is more frightening and daunting than actually finding them. Potential cash suppliers can turn up where you least expect them. A good place to begin your cash search is to network with business colleagues, family, friends, and acquaintances. It's important to get the word out that you're looking for investors for real estate deals. You may run up against dead ends in your immediate circle, so your cash quest should extend well beyond your comfort zone. When I first started out, as I talked about earlier, I used hard-money lenders. Then, as I networked with other investors and discovered who the private investors were in my markets, I began to use their money to do my deals. You can, too.

Title and real estate companies also may know of and be willing to share the names of private lenders. If you have the right credit or collateral, some of these individuals may cooperate with you and be willing to give you a short-term loan. Get used to people saying no, though, especially if you're a new investor. But eventually you'll be able to find several cash options. Also check your local Yellow Pages for "money brokers" or "mortgage brokers" and follow up with a phone call to learn more. Of course, you'll have to screen any potential investor. But this networking and research will get you started.

LOOKING FOR HARD-MONEY LENDERS?

If you're in the market for hard-money lenders, a good resource or place to start is JeffAdamsLenders (www.jeffadamslenders.com). Remember, I had no money when I started and was on the verge of bankruptcy. Then the investor, who wanted to sell me that first REO property on Sepulveda Avenue in San Bernardino, introduced me to hard-money lenders. That's how I secured the money to buy my first REOs. I used cash advances on my credit cards to buy the paint and supplies to fix up the houses that I eventually flipped to other buyers for profits. As I did more deals and paid off my debts, I began building profits so I could start stockpiling my own investing cash while still working full-time as a fireman.

Partnering for Cash

My first deals without using my own cash were 15 years ago. Times and the economy have changed, but absolutely you can still do the same thing today whether using cash from hard-money lenders, private investors, or your own money. That's one of the big advantages of REO investing—you can start with no cash of your own and build real estate investing success one deal at a time. Alex Galitsky, the Belarus native who immigrated to this country and eventually ended up in central Florida as a Realtor, started that way—one small deal at a time, building cash as he went. So did Zack Childress and Yunona Hagopjanian, a California mother of two, and hundreds more like them all across the country.

"If someone doesn't have cash but they have time, they need to find somebody who does have cash and pair up with them . . . be it a hard-money lender or just a private investor or private lender," says Galitsky, who today doesn't use his own cash for REO deals. Instead, he finds and expedites REO purchases for a pool of investors, and takes a finder's fee or commission on each deal. It's a smaller paycheck, but one with no risk on his part, and he makes up the difference with the high volume of deals.

IRA Funds

To finance his first real estate investment property, Eugene Seagriff, the Lehigh Valley, Pennsylvania, investor, tapped into his self-directed individual retirement account (IRA) and seller financing. It was an IRA he had funded through a 401(k) in a previous job, and amounted to enough to take care of various owner issues and bring the house up to code. Proceeds from the property's sale would be enough to repay the note to the property's former owner. That approach to financing appealed to Seagriff because he didn't need much cash for the deal, and then he wouldn't have to pay any interest charges on the money. Seagriff accessed his home's equity for the down payment and closing costs. Unfortunately, lending requirements changed drastically while in the process of purchasing the multi-unit property, and at the last minute he needed additional cash for the deal. Luckily (and calculatedly so) he had a backup plan, and he partnered with someone who had the cash. His partner was a friend of the family. "It turns out good people you know have money," Seagriff says. "The first place you go is folks in your circle. You would be surprised how much capital is available."

That first deal gave Seagriff the confidence he needed. The money is out there; you simply have to look for it. You can do it, too! It was pretty simple for Seagriff to line up more investors for his next purchase.

It's the strategy of one deal at a time that builds and builds and builds your confidence, your skill, and your business.

Friends and Family

In Seagriff's case, the initial investor partner—the family friend— found out about the real estate venture from one of Seagriff's relatives. Another friend of the friend subsequently heard of the investment opportunity and came on board to purchase a second rental property. Joining in conversations about real estate and mentioning what he was doing to others, and suddenly Seagriff found himself with a consortium of four investors, and together they had enough capital to get started buying, rehabbing, and then flipping REOs. Such is the power of perseverance and networking with family and friends.

Getting cash from friends and family isn't always that easy. Alabama investor Zack Childress attests to that. He tried the family route first, but in the beginning everyone said no. Many, many successes to his credit later, he says everyone wants to give him money to invest now. "But not in the beginning," he adds. "They thought I was crazy to think I could make money investing in real estate."

One Deal at a Time

Californian Yunona Hagopjanian started with no money, but she stayed focused and developed her business. It wasn't easy even to find people who could answer her questions, she says. But she learned all she could about the process, grew her business, and became successful. In the beginning it was one small deal at a time.

Real Estate Investors Associations

Another former student, successful real estate investor, and former mentor/coach with my program is Gerald Lucas. His advice to new investors who want to develop funding sources and more is to find and attend meetings of local real estate investment clubs. These consist of real estate investors—new and experienced—and others who organize groups to network and to further their real estate knowledge. That's where Lucas picked up referrals for specific hard-money lenders he still uses today. Check out the National Real Estate Investors Association website (www.nationalreia.com) and use its "Find an REIA" tool to locate clubs in your target market. Then go to the meetings (usually once a week or once a month at a local restaurant or conference center) and network. Ask other investors for good hard-money lenders.

Other online sources to find your local real estate investor clubs include:

- Creative Real Estate Online (www.creonline.com). Type "real estate clubs" into its search tool, and it will bring up more than 100 references to listings in various states and more.

- Google (www.google.com). **Google "real estate investor clubs" for thousands of listings.**
- BiggerPockets.com (www.biggerpockets.com/real-estate-investment-clubs.html). **Use this site's search tool, which allows you to find clubs by state.**

Banks and Mortgage Lenders

> Hard-money lenders make cash loans based on the value of the property—the collateral—while banks and mortgages tend to base a loan on the borrower's income and creditworthiness.

Beginning REO investors often are more likely to turn to hard-money lenders or creative financing than to banks and mortgage lenders to fund their early deals. There are several reasons why.

REO investing takes a bundle of quick cash up front, and that doesn't leave much wiggle room to finesse a loan from a bank, let alone a mortgage lender. Banks and mortgage lenders tend to make loans based on an individual's creditworthiness or income. Not only may a beginning REO investor fail to qualify for those loans, but the process can be so arduous, tedious, and lengthy that even if an investor qualifies, the deal has long since evaporated.

Hard-money lenders, on the other hand, generally lend cash based on the value of the collateral—in this case a property. If a hard-money lender finds a deal appealing, an REO investor can have cash in hand very quickly.

That doesn't mean an REO investor should slam the door on either banks or mortgage lenders as potential sources of cash, however. Long-term relationships with both are a necessity. They may be able to provide potential properties for purchase. You'll also need one or both to negotiate long-term loans for properties with an exit strategy of buy and hold.

For a beginning investor with good credit, a bank also may be willing to advance cash for a deal as a signature, short-term loan, especially with the promise of more of your business ahead. Banks, after all, are in the business of loaning money. That's how they make their money. The key is for an investor to convincingly show a risk-averse bank that a short-term signature loan will net them sizable profits.

If you as an investor can show a bank you are successful at buying and holding or buying and flipping properties and you have the collateral to prove it, a routine will develop so that when you find a deal, you simply call your banker to advance you the fast cash. That's a primary financing approach I take today.

HOW TO SCREEN A LENDER

All cash sources are not created equal. Just because someone makes a promise or says they'll do something, doesn't mean it will happen. Therefore, as with any other business dealing, it's necessary to screen any potential lenders. Your reputation is at stake. If a lender doesn't deliver on the cash as promised and a deal falls through as a result, all the property's seller (the bank or REO agent) cares about is that you can't be counted on to follow through with a deal.

Make the Calls

We've described the importance of networking with real estate investors, your professional team, and others to identify potential cash sources. A referral is the best approach, but it's not always possible to get one. Once you do have a referral or have found an individual or a group through the Yellow Pages, online research, or classified ads, you'll need to call and ask questions to get a clearer picture of who the lender is, what the lender can offer, and what the lender's track record looks like. Don't be nervous about making these calls. As an investor you represent potential profits to a lender.

A sample way to begin the conversation:

> Hi. My name is [Jeff Adams]. I buy bank-owned properties and fix them up, and then sell or hold on to them as rentals. I'm looking to fund my deals, so I wanted to see if I could work with you. Do you mind if I ask you a few questions?

The Right Approach

Always be upbeat. Smile as you're talking and you'll come across in a more positive manner. Be polite and businesslike, too. This is, after all, a business where first impressions happen fast and count plenty. Don't be discouraged if lots of potential lenders say no. That's the nature of the business. Remember, too, that the goal isn't just to find money; it's also to get a good idea of whether a lender is willing to work with you. You haven't identified any properties yet, anyway, and lenders generally won't give out money on the terms you need until they first see the details of a specific deal. You'll need to find a number of different lenders so that you have plenty of Plan B options in case a particular lender passes on a deal or backs out at the last minute—and one or more will, that's a guarantee.

Ask Questions

Some questions to ask a potential money source, depending on whether it's a private lender, a mortgage broker, or someone else entirely, include:

- What percentage of a deal can you finance?
- Can you lend against the appraised value rather than the purchase price?
- Will you allow the seller to quitclaim the property to me so I can refinance it? (A quitclaim is a deed by which the grantor gives up any claim he may have in the property.)
- Do you have hard money to lend against rehabs?
- Do you do stated-income or no-doc lending? (The latter refers to no documentation of income or credit.)

When it comes to loan officers or mortgage brokers—be sure to speak with the actual loan officer or broker and not an assistant—some questions to ask include:

- How many different lenders do you work with at present? (Most mom-and-pop shops work with only about 15 or 20 lenders;

usually 2 or 3 of those are willing to work with investors. That can limit the amount of business they'll do with you, and slow down how fast you grow your business unless you have other funding sources.)

- What types of loan products do you offer that can help me as an investor? (These can include stated-income loans, no-doc loans, adjustable rate mortgages, negative amortization loans, and bridge loans.)
- Do you have 100 percent financing available?
- Do you have loan products that you lend against the appraised value of a property or the purchase price?
- Do you offer creative financing? Do you have private investors, and hard money?
- Do you have any equity lenders?
- Do you have fix-up loans?
- Is the loan based on my income or on the property itself?
- What is the maximum number of loans you will make to the same borrower concurrently?

RED FLAG WARNING

If a lender wants cash up front to talk to you or before he or she will discuss details of a particular deal, move on. Chances are that's not the kind of cash source—if indeed it is a cash source—you want or need.

HOW TO PERSUADE A LENDER TO WORK WITH YOU

Ideally, an REO investor would like to have a group of stable lenders who are repeat customers—waiting in the wings, cash in hand for the next deal and the next and so on. That's not a pipe dream. That's possible and plausible if you take the right approach; if you're professional, credible, honest, and straightforward in your dealings; and if you know where to go and how to structure your deals.

It all starts with the phone call, then the follow-up and more follow-up, then the right presentation of a deal. Image backed by action is everything in this business. That means you personally need to look professional and any REO deal packet you present to a bank or potential lender should look professional, too.

Dress the part. If you're a free spirit, that's okay, but if you want the deal, look professional and impressive. A suit is ideal, but if that's not in your financial cards right now, consider wearing a "company uniform." That could be a nice pair of slacks and a polo shirt embroidered with your company's name. The embroidery costs only a few dollars and definitely adds professionalism and legitimacy to your company— whether you've done your first deal or not.

When it comes to lending money, decision makers like to see the details of a potential deal, especially if you're a beginning investor. A few pieces of advice (we talk more about the paperwork in Chapter 13):

- Make the request for money in writing, and print it clearly on good-quality paper stock.
- Include an introductory/cover letter—who you are, what you do, what you want the money for, how you intend to repay the money; repair estimates; quality photographs of the property; and a portfolio of past projects (if you have any).
- Include a copy of the completed (still tentative) contract as verification the deal is real. Use a photocopy because you'll be sending the proposal to several potential lenders at the same time.
- Include comparable sales reports. In the hard-money lending business, the value of the property means everything. Be sure to calculate and include the property's future market value, and make sure the lender is aware of that.
- Place the information in a binder as opposed to a folder or loose pages. A binder looks more professional.
- Don't present the information in a sloppy manner. Make sure all the grammar and spelling is correct in the documents. Again, it's about first impressions.

EXAMPLE OF A COVER LETTER TO A POTENTIAL LENDER*

Dear [Name of Lender]:

We wish to request a loan in the amount of $85,000 with a term of no greater than one year for the purchase of a single-family residence located at 321 Sycamore Avenue, Mudville, Florida. Our business buys bank-owned properties (REOs) and then rehabilitates and resells them. The property in question is owned by ABC Bank. It currently is vacant.

Our research indicates that the subject property will have a fair market value of $140,000 to $150,000 after we complete the repairs. The estimate is based on comparable sales reports, copies of which are included with this packet. Our estimates include repair costs of $10,000, which includes the cost of modernizing the bathrooms, replacing the flooring throughout, painting the interior walls, and replacing roof shingles.

We have negotiated a price of $75,000 from the bank. The remainder of the funding we are requesting from you will be used for improvements and repairs to the property. We've included a spreadsheet detailing the use of funds for the project. We expect the repairs and improvements to take approximately 30 days to complete. Comparable homes in the area have been selling within 45 days, so we expect to pay the full amount of this loan within 90 days of receipt of the cash.

We will be happy to meet with you personally to answer any questions you might have. You can contact me at [888-888-8888].

Thank you for your time and consideration in this matter. Sincerely,

[Your signature]

*For a downloadable, customizable version of this letter that you can personalize for your needs, please visit www.jeffadamsforms.com

About Points

A point is basically a commission that a borrower pays to a lender for the use of the lender's money. One point equals 1 percent of a loan's value. In many cases, points are negotiable. An investor with good credit may be able to get a loan for 1 to 2 points with the point payment spread out—1 point up front and 1 at the back end of a deal.

For someone with subprime, poor, or challenged credit, money still is available but the points are higher—perhaps 5 points. Some hard-money lenders may even want to charge double-digit points. If that's the case, look for another lender.

A simple way to calculate the cost of points is to move the decimal point at the end of your purchase price or the price of the money you borrow two digits to the left, and then multiply by the number of points. For example, if an investor borrows $25,000 at 1 point, 1 percent of $25,000 equals $250. At 2 points, it's $500 and so on.

COMMON REAL ESTATE FINANCING TERMS

- **Rate:** What banks and other lenders charge for the money they lend. The rate includes costs like points, non-owner-occupied fees, prepayment penalty buy-down fees, and other costs that add up to the annual percentage rate (APR).

- **Points:** Basically, a commission charged to you; usually negotiable. One point is 1 percent of the loan amount (for example, 1 percent of $100,000 equals $1,000).
- **Front-end/back-end fees:** Front-end fees usually are paid at the closing of a deal or in the beginning, although it's possible to negotiate to pay some of the front-end costs at the back end of the deal. Back-end fees are those paid when the loan is paid off, usually after the property has been flipped.

Chapter 6

HOW TO RESEARCH YOUR MARKET, CREATE AN INVESTING PLAN, AND DEVELOP AN EXIT STRATEGY

*If you want to know where the market [growth] is going, follow the
sewer lines.*
        **—Zack Childress, successful real estate investor and Jeff
                Adams, Foreclosure Academy instructor**

Would-be successful REO investors, especially beginners, must
know and understand their playing field—the target market
area in which they want to invest. The best pennies-on-the-dollar deal
is a bust if it's in the wrong place at the wrong time with the wrong surroundings. "Location, location, location" is the mantra of real estate
investing. But if your plan is to buy and flip or hold properties, you
also need to know what's happening in the surrounding area now and
what's expected in the future, including details about the neighborhoods; the state of the job market; the quality of the schools; physical
access to the area, including major thoroughfares and public transpor-
tation; property values; resale values; pricing ups and downs and highs
and lows; competition; hot spots (and cold ones); crime statistics; and
local market demands.

That's a lot to learn, but the financial rewards are well worth it.

FOCUS, FOCUS, FOCUS

In Part I, we discussed the importance of conviction and positive
thinking to develop your successful REO business. Your ability to
focus plays a big role, too. You must focus—not only on what it takes
to get the job done but also on a specific target market. Focus is the
opposite of trying to make a deal on any kind of property, in any location, and in any way possible. If you don't focus, you could flounder
without ever making a deal, or you could make one deal and never
make another. As mentioned earlier, when I first started out, I was
looking all over the place for properties without a particular target or
exit strategy—and I couldn't make a single deal. It wasn't until I
focused my energies on one specific area with a specific exit strategy—

buying, repairing, and flipping the properties—that I began to make deals successfully. Even after years of successful real estate investing, today I primarily concentrate my investing in only four counties in my market. If you're just beginning, try two counties—or even one!

Before ever investing a dime, invest time and energy into researching the best region, county, or neighborhoods in which to concentrate your efforts, and then find the ideal exit strategy to meet your investing needs. Even if you don't have investing experience, it's vitally important to know the market and the background of your investment area before you approach a bank or an REO agent about a deal. Such knowledge adds to your credibility and professionalism, and will go a long way toward swaying a bank or agent to accept you as a serious contender.

How to Find the Best Area

Perhaps there's a fortune to be made in your own backyard or somewhere in the surrounding area. The only way to know is to do the research. That's how Eugene Seagriff determined that Lehigh Valley, Pennsylvania—near the New York/New Jersey area in which he lives—had great real estate potential and how he decided on it as the market for his investing efforts. Remember, in Chapter 3 Seagriff talked about the area's great job opportunities and its location at the intersection of major highways—factors that make it a relatively solid area for him to buy and hold rental property. Another positive aspect of the area is that prices of properties there are far more reasonable than in New York or New Jersey, where Seagriff lives.

Critical data concerning real estate markets for various areas are available from websites like RealtyTrac (www.realtytrac.com) and CoreLogic's RealQuest (www.realquest.com).

Where to Start

If you plan to invest in an area some distance away, you might consider starting out on the Internet to give yourself some background about various locales. Google the name of the county, city, town, municipality, or whatever area you're interested in, and start reading about what's happening there. Check out local blogs and e-zines as well as newspapers to get an idea of developments concerning properties, the arts, education, crime, the business community, and jobs in the area.

Questions to ask and issues to consider about the area include:

- Is the employment picture in the area solid? Are new employers coming in or old ones going out? If the latter is the case, you'll need to research the trend further. Job flight doesn't bode well for the possibility of newcomers (property buyers and renters) moving into an area. And you can't cash a profit check unless you flip the property or rent it to someone.
- Find the nearest chamber of commerce and contact it for information about retail and development in the area.
- Research the local schools. Do they have a solid reputation? Schools are important if your exit strategy involves first-time homebuyers and/or renters who might have young children. (Incidentally, those homebuyers can be a great target market for smaller, affordable properties.)
- What, if anything, will attract newcomers to an area?
- Is there a college or university nearby and, if so, could students or teachers be your target renters/buyers?
- Call the local police or sheriff's department to find out about a specific area's crime rate. It's important to stay away from "war zones." The reasons are twofold: poor resale potential and possible theft or vandalism. I once bought a property that I thought was a great deal. If I had done my homework, I would have realized otherwise. We had to rehab it several times before we could finally flip it because thieves kept stripping out the copper and anything and everything else of value.

Keep in mind, too, that a newer area of a town may not necessarily be the best area on which to concentrate your time and efforts. There may be plenty of REOs in newer areas, but often the job picture in those places has deteriorated to the point at which it may be difficult to flip or rent houses there.

Familiar Territory

You may consider beginning your REO investing in a geographic area you already know something about or have some familiarity with. Getting started and researching the details can be simpler if you already have contacts there. Conversely, don't hesitate to move on to another area if, in doing your due diligence, you recognize strong drawbacks to investing in an area. Another option for your investing might be an up-and-coming area or an economically strong area with a high employment rate.

RED FLAG WARNING

When considering a target area or property, ask yourself: "Would I want to live here? Why or Why not?" If the answer is "No, not ever, not under any circumstance," then the kind of buyer or renter you would like to have (as in reliable and dependable) might not want to live there, either. Walk away from the potential area or deal!

The Next Step

Once you've narrowed your focus somewhat, another aspect of researching a market is to look for the hot and cold areas. *Hot* areas equal investor activity and regular inventory that moves at predictable price points. You can find much of this information by contacting title companies or searching various databases in person or online, including in most cases the county recorder's office (every county has property records that are public). You want to find out where the most homes have sold and what the general price ranges have been. You can talk to real estate brokers and check the MLS to find where the most sales are occurring. Other third-party websites that can help are

RealQuest (www.realquest.com), Zillow (www.zillow.com), and Redfin (www.redfin.com).

The Map Approach

This may sound like a grade school exercise, but buy a map of the general area where you hope to concentrate your investing efforts and put it up on a corkboard on the wall. When you learn something—positive or negative—about a specific neighborhood or area, write it on a piece of paper and stick-pin it to the map. That way you'll know at a glance what's going on. (We'll use this same map later when it comes to pricing properties to buy and sell.) When you buy a property as an investor with the help of the map and the research it displays, you'll also get a good idea of the salability of a particular property. Ideally, you should concentrate your efforts in desirable neighborhoods.

Exit Strategy and Approach

To come out a winner with REO investing requires quick deal-making and efficient execution of the exit strategy—what you plan to do with the property once you buy it. We all want to make money, but there are multiple ways to accomplish that, all of which involve execution of a planned strategy. Whether the economy is up or down, multiple exit strategies are available, depending on your personal situation, the financing you have available, your short- and long-term goals, and more. In the beginning, as I learned, it's best to focus your energies on one exit strategy. Then, once you have some experience, you can branch out to multiple exit strategies.

Although we detail the various exit strategies later in the book, let's briefly review the powerful primary exit options available with REOs:

- **Buy and flip the property at retail on the open market, typically to first-time homebuyers.** Many potential homebuyers have been sitting on the sidelines, unsure whether to buy and often deciding not to buy because of prices or loan concerns.

Now, as interest rates remain at or near all-time lows and prices are affordable, those people are making their move. Later in the book we talk more about government-assisted affordable housing programs and how you can take advantage of those.

- **Buy the property, hold it briefly, and then sell it at a wholesale price to other investors.** That means at a reduced price off the after-repair value (ARV). You won't make as much money on the deal, but it's quick and easy with little or no risk to you.
- **Buy and hold the property as a rental.** This approach often can mean an instant regular income stream if a property you buy already has tenants. If the property is vacant, some repair probably will be needed before you can rent it out, but after fix-up and once it's rented, it will provide a regular income. My annual income from rental properties is more than $200,000.

What Exit Strategy Works for You?

To help determine what will work best for you, start by asking yourself a few questions:

- **Are you planning to invest part-time or full-time?** If you're interested in investing to supplement your income from another full-time job, you may want to consider buying, holding, and renting out your property for guaranteed monthly income. On the other end of the spectrum, buying and flipping a property to a wholesaler can be a fast way to generate cash without the head-ache of long-term property ownership. Profits tend to be smaller with wholesale flips, but these kinds of REO deals are quick and clean. If you develop a group of investors with cash to spend and the right contacts, the deals can be consistent and require very little work. The other alternative is to buy, repair, and flip prop-erties for profit. That's how I got started, but in the beginning I also did a lot of the repair work myself. If you're not the handy-man type or don't want to take that kind of hands-on approach, that strategy probably isn't right for you.

- **Who is your target audience?** Are you targeting first-time buyers? Are you planning to wholesale properties to other investors? If you're considering buying and holding a property as a rental, who's your target renter—low-income workers or professionals, singles or families? The answers to these questions will affect the type of investment property and its location.
- **How much cash will you likely have to invest? For how long?** The cash pit isn't bottomless for beginners or seasoned investors, so you'll need to set a dollar cap on a deal and not exceed it without your investors' approval.
- **What strategy works well in the current economy?** Overall economic conditions should factor into your decision on an exit strategy. For example, if as an investor you were looking to make substantial profits when housing markets were at their peak several years ago, the better approach would have been to buy and flip immediately rather than buy and hold. Today, when prices are near bottom, it can make more sense to buy and hold a property as a rental. That can generate regular monthly income today while you hold the property to sell later when values rise.

My exit strategy as of mid-2011 called for buying up REOs and holding them as rental properties until the market rebounds, and then selling off some of those properties. Floridian and successful real estate investor Chris McLaughlin agrees with the buy-and-hold strategy. He already holds more than 140 properties and is a very active buyer. In February 2011 alone, he bought 10 more properties. When the market rebounds, he'll consider selling them, but in the meantime they generate a positive monthly cash flow.

OUTSIDE ADVICE AND EXPERTISE

Investing in REOs is not about reinventing the wheel. Plenty of people have learned the right way to buy and sell or hold REO properties successfully for the long term. You as a new investor must learn to listen to the winners and tune out both the losers and the spectators. In the pages of this book, I'm giving you the framework you need to succeed, but the rest is up to you. (You can also check out my free seven-day e-course on real estate investing at www.freerealestatementoring.com.)

Real estate investing is a business of continuing education. Experts, myself included, will tell you that the more you learn about it, the better you'll be at it. Aside from reading as many books and listening to as many tapes as possible, take advantage of conferences and boot camps. Join real estate investment groups, and listen to the seminars and webinars available from reputable people. Use these tools as networking opportunities if nothing else. The beauty of CDs and DVDs—my REO Riches program is available in both formats—is that you can learn at your own speed.

The Importance of a Mentor

Often an outgrowth of networking in any field is that you find one individual who really helps you, who is a sounding board for your ideas and approaches, and a stalwart with good advice. That person is a mentor. REO investing is no different. In fact, a mentor can be especially important when it comes to helping you learn the right way to structure deals for optimum profit.

This also is a business where it pays to learn from others' mistakes. The right mentor should be able to steer you in the right direction to avoid many of the bumps and roadblocks along your road to successful deals. (For your free one-on-one consultation, visit www.REIsuccessCoach.com).

A Note of Caution

Whether you're looking for a mentor or even a guru with information that's valuable to your growth and success, watch out for the pseudo experts. They abound in real estate.

RED FLAG WARNING

Choose your mentors and coaches carefully. Simply doing a few REO deals does not qualify a person as an REO expert.

Be careful of any real estate "experts" who want cash up front before they will talk to you or who ask for cash to enter their websites. Any reputable teacher should offer free webinars, free trials, and money-back guarantees.

Chapter 7

HOW TO GET READY FOR YOUR FIRST DEAL AND BUILD CREDIBILITY

Your credibility is on the line before, during, and after any potential deal. Wise investors act accordingly.

— **Jeff Adams**

To build your REO business, you must build your credibility as a dependable professional who makes deals happen. The process means marketing yourself as the go-to buyer who does what he or she says they'd do and wraps up good deals quickly and efficiently, deal after deal. It also means having an equally efficient, knowledgeable, and professional team of experts behind you—your power team. Your professionalism and theirs helps to create your long-term success because the goal, after all, is to have the best REO deals come to you. And they will—even as you're just beginning your REO business—if you have done your homework and have a professional approach and follow-through.

Remember the three Ps of real estate: people, properties, and processes. What you do before, during, and after a deal—and the professionalism and efficiency with which you approach that and any other potential deal, as well as your honesty and up-front approach—will help establish your credibility. That credibility will help develop you as the go-to or pocket buyer real estate agents want to have at their fingertips. From your point of view—and theirs—that means repeat business. Wouldn't it be great if once a month, once a week, or daily you opened your e-mail in-box, checked your fax machine, or picked up the telephone to find a list of great deals for your taking? It can and does happen regularly to ordinary people like you.

Honest and Up Front

To build credibility in this business, as in any business, you must do what you say you'll do. It's very simple. If you promise to do something, do it. If you tell a broker you will fax an offer in the afternoon, fax the offer that afternoon. If you make an offer on a property and the offer is accepted, follow through and close the deal. If you don't make good on your promises—explicit and implied—you'll quickly get the reputation that working with you is a waste of time, and your offers will end up in the trash. Real estate agents don't get paid until a deal is complete.

Be aboveboard and open about how you plan to complete a deal; what type of financing you will use (hard-money financing or some other approach); and how you plan to take title. Real estate agents, banks, lenders, and others involved don't like surprises, especially when large sums of money are involved.

Pay Attention to the Laws

Make sure anything you do or promise to do is legal in your particular state or market. That may sound elementary, but too often in the real estate business, people try to get away with shady dealings. The truth is that even if it may be possible to stretch or bend the laws a bit, there's usually a legal way to accomplish the same end. It may simply take a bit longer. But being beyond reproach can differentiate you from plenty of others out there, further establishing your credibility in the process.

Every state is its own country when it comes to real estate closing rules and regulations. The laws may sound similar, but they're likely different in some way. If some aspect of your approach isn't legal, that's a quick way to torpedo a deal with no recourse for you. Worse, you'll get the wrong kind of reputation. People don't want to work with those who could jeopardize their jobs.

To help ensure that your deals comply with the letter of the law, you must research the pertinent state and local laws. Know the laws in your own state and in any other state where you do business, and make sure your power team knows them, too. Online or in person, check out your state's department or board of real estate, the entity that licenses and monitors real estate agents and transactions. Another good source of information is a local or state bar association. Their websites generally include links to state and local real estate laws. Plenty of other websites tout "real estate laws." It's fine to check them out, but don't assume that what you read on these sites is always correct or up-to-date unless they provide links to the latest information on government websites. It's far better to check directly with the entity in charge of enforcing the laws of your particular state or locality.

Educate Yourself

Knowledge is key in this business. The more you know—the more familiar you are with all parts of the REO investing process—the better you will be in the business and the more profits you will make. If you don't understand something or are confused by an aspect of the process, seek help. Look to mentors, educators, and experts in a particular field. As we've talked about, learn about your target market, too. (For a free 30-minute consultation from me, visit www.REIsuccessCoach.com).

If you're not an expert at rehabbing homes (and even if you are), spend a day at your local home improvement superstore. Look around, price various home repairs and replacements, and keep a record of that pricing. Find out the average price per square foot for average carpet; the cost of painting a home's exterior and interior; how much it costs to replace doors, windows, toilets, and sinks. Price the mid- to low-grade products, not the high-end ones. The goal when investing in rehabs is to bring a property up to comparable and competitive standards, and not to exceed them. It's usually better to find out local prices as opposed to checking prices online or from home improvement websites because prices can vary widely by geographic area.

Get to know the salespeople in the contractor department in these stores, too. They can be a wealth of help to you now and in the future. Let them know that you'll bring them regular business. The goal is to eventually be able to pick up the phone, call them, and get a fast estimate on a repair price. They may also be able to provide a price list of general products. That can help expedite your ability to determine the approximate cost to repair a potential property, and in turn make the right offer to buy that property. Some of the stores also will offer contractor discounts and special coupons for people in the business.

YOUR POWER TEAM

When I first started out, one of my mentors told me it was imperative that I find and build relationships with a core group of specialists— from termite inspectors to title companies, lenders, appraisers, escrow companies (or closing attorneys, depending on the laws of your state), Realtors, REO agents, and more. These experts in their individual fields would then become the power team that I could count on to get things done when I needed them done. You, too, must find and develop your own power team of independent professionals because no one—no matter how much they know—can be an expert in every-thing. Deals happen as a result of a group of professionals who know their business and work together. The profitable side effect of a team of your own is that any one of them will step out of their comfort zone and go the extra mile to make sure the role they play in your deal is done right. That's what having your own power team is all about. It's not the "power" aspect of the equation that counts; it's the "team" part that nets results. The key is to develop relationships with these independent professionals so that you become the first in line to get something done when it must be done. These professionals in the business also can be great sources of referrals to other experts in dif-ferent fields.

I've used the same escrow and title company for more than 12 years. If I have to, I can call and tell them that a deal needs to be done in three days, and it will get done. Typically when an investor has a deal in escrow (or with a closing attorney—depending on how your state handles property closings), generally he or she has to babysit that deal—follow up continuously—until it's done. With an investor-friendly escrow and title company (or closing attorney) on your power team, they often can keep tabs on the deal for you.

Let's look more closely at some of the most important members of your power team.

Realtor/Real Estate Agent

A real estate agent is your link to deals and your connection to the Multiple Listing Service (MLS). Look for a good Realtor or agent who is willing to listen and who knows and understands the local market. Some real estate agents may be reluctant to work with investors, often because they really don't understand the business. If that's the case, explain to the agent what you plan to do—provide him or her a fast and easy way to close all-cash deals—and how your plan can increase his or her income significantly. Because agents work on commission, if an investor brings them regular deals, then that translates into regular and steady commissions.

If you follow through and show an agent that, as promised, you close deals quickly and easily and with all cash—which saves the time and hassle of mortgage lenders—he or she will quickly come to you first with the best potential deals.

When searching for the right Realtor, look for an agent with experience dealing with REOs. The best way to do that is to contact large real estate brokerages. A seasoned Realtor in a major brokerage may not be willing to work with a beginning investor, but talk to the brokerage anyway and ask to meet with their newest agent with REO experience. Chances are, newer agents will be hungry for new business and embrace the opportunity to work with someone who can bring them multiple closings in a short time.

A note of caution regarding the right Realtor: It's important that an agent understand and have experience writing REO offers, as well as know exactly what you're looking for in terms of properties, locations, and requirements.

The right agent also can help with property repair estimates, evictions, price evaluation of comparable properties, and more. Any agent on your team needs to take the job and you seriously. If not, move on and find someone else.

Mortgage Lender/Hard-Money Lenders

It's essential to include several different mortgage lenders and hard-money lenders on your power team in order to have options and backups should you need them. In choosing your team members, ask each potential candidate the following questions:

- Are you willing to lend money to investors?
- Will you lend against appraised value as opposed to purchase price? Lending against appraised value indicates that the lender may come up with all the cash necessary to purchase and repair a property.
- Will you put together 100 percent financing packages? This means the lender can get all the money from several sources without your paying anything out of pocket.
- Do you have hard money to lend? This cash comes from private investors rather than lending institutions.
- Can you do stated-income, no-doc (no documentation of income), or nonverified lending? In this case, the lender will look at certain aspects of the deal other than your credit and income. Even if you have bad credit, no credit, or no income, the lender will work with you if you have a sure moneymaking deal.

A starting place to find the right professional is the website for the National Association of Mortgage Brokers (www.namb.org), which has a search tool that allows you to find members by city and state as well as links to state and local organizations of professionals. Realtors and other investors also can provide references to lenders. As mentioned earlier, Real Estate Investment Association (REIA) members and other successful investors are excellent sources of referrals, too.

Banker

If you have good credit, a bank can be your link to fast money. Your eventual goal as an REO investor is to be able to get a signature loan for fast cash to buy a property, flip the property, and then quickly pay back the cash. If you don't have credit right now, don't fret it. As you develop your successful business, the good credit will follow.

In the meantime, start today by getting to know a bank vice president who has lending authority. Avoid the giant money center banks, and instead look for small local and community banks. Find out who at the bank handles real estate investment loans, and introduce yourself. Don't pitch your company, but find out what kinds of real estate deals might interest the bank, and ask about their lending guidelines. Interview the appropriate vice presidents at many banks, and let them know that you plan to bring them repeat business. Despite the money crunch of recent years in the wake of the subprime meltdown, some smaller banks have begun to loosen their lending purse strings. These banks may have money for small community (reinvestment) loans that could enable you to rehab properties as rentals or to then sell them to first-time homebuyers. These loans are designed to promote the community, while boosting the banks' business. Ask about them. Also find out if a bank offers a blanket loan—one loan that can be used for multiple properties.

Banks also can be good sources for finding REO agents who control the bank-owned inventory in your market.

Title Company

Title companies check out property records to verify ownership of real estate, usually prior to buying and selling of the property, then issue title certificates as verification of clear title. In some cases, a title company also can act as the independent third party that handles property closings.

For an investor, an established relationship with a title company can mean the possibility of title reports for free or a nominal charge because the company knows that the investor will bring them lots of business. I've worked closely with the Title and Insurance Services division of First American Financial Corporation (www.firstam.com) for 15 years, and because I'm a frequent customer, they give me a discount on my title policies. For example, the average person sells a home every five years and pays approximately $1,000 for title insurance on that sale. I pay only $650 per title and get access to running property profiles and comparable values on properties through their FASTWeb online system (https://fwprodweb1.firstam.com/fastweb/home.asp). A number of other title companies are under the umbrella of Fidelity National Financial, including Commonwealth Land Title

Insurance Company (www.cltic.com), and Lawyers Title (www.ltic. com), which has access to the Nite Owl online system—another database for running property profiles and comparables.

As an investor (and potential frequent customer), contact the title company you would like to do business with, tell them you're an investor who will be bringing them regular and frequent business, and ask for a discount on their services as well as access to run property profiles and comparable pricing data.

RED FLAG WARNING

If a title company is not willing to work with you and accommodate your needs as a real estate investor, look elsewhere.

Realtors are great sources for title company referrals. Make sure, though, that any company you use is experienced in REOs and understands the nuances of flipping properties quickly if that's your exit strategy.

Escrow Company

Some states use escrow companies; others require closing attorneys to close deals. An escrow company's job is to act as a neutral third party between buyer and seller to make sure all aspects of a contract are carried out. In an REO, the escrow company or closing attorney acts between the bank and you (or whoever is designated as the investor) and is involved in transferring the documents, money, title insurance, and more. Essential to your power team, this company also needs to be investor-friendly and familiar with how REO investing works. As we've mentioned, REOs can involve out-of-the-norm title transfers.

To find an escrow company, talk to Realtors, banks, lenders, REO agents, title companies, and other investors for referrals. The American

Escrow Association (www.a-e-a.org), the trade association of the settlement industry, offers more helpful information on its website.

Real Estate Closing Attorney

Some states require a real estate closing attorney rather than an escrow
company to close a deal. Referrals are one way to find the best attorney
for your team. Again, talk to title companies, REIAs, and real estate
investors. Local bar associations are another source of information.
Make sure any attorney you use has real estate expertise, and prefera-
bly experience with real estate investors.

You don't need to hire the top partner in a law firm at $500 an hour.
As with real estate agents, ask to speak with the newest hire. It will cost
significantly less and will work well as long as the new lawyer has real
estate and title experience.

Accountant/CPA

Income taxes and capital gains related to buying and selling real estate
can be complicated. It's important to discuss tax strategies with someone who understands their impact. Look for a certified public accountant (CPA) with an understanding of real estate investing, which does
require special expertise. If certain deals aren't structured properly,
you could end up with significant tax consequences. Ask CPAs for
referrals to Realtors and brokers.

Handyman/Rehab Specialist

When it comes to rehabbing or repairing a property for sale or rent, a
professional handyman or rehab specialist is priceless. He or she
should be able to do quality work—shabby work can quickly kill a
potential deal—at reasonable prices. Look for someone who is reliable
and can act as your general contractor if you decide to rehab the property. Your handyman should be able to quickly estimate property rehab
and/or repair costs.

THE QUEST FOR YOUR TEAM MEMBERS

Whether you're a beginner or a seasoned pro, approach the search for your team members with professionalism and courtesy. Ask pertinent questions, be forthcoming, and stay in control. In most cases you will need a team made up of several individuals in each field of expertise. One lender isn't enough—you'll need several, just as one title company or one handyman isn't enough, either. You need backup plans in case of unforeseen glitches (and they will happen, no matter how thorough you are), and your team needs players who can and will come off the bench and contribute.

Look for Referrals

One of the best sources of potential experts for your power team is referrals from other professionals, whether investors, banks, Realtors, REO agents, title companies, or attorneys. Other successful REO investors are a great source, too. Every contact you make is a potential referral source. If you approach someone about a deal or a proposal, and that person can't or won't or doesn't care to work with you on that project, don't walk away until you ask, "Do you know someone else who might be able to help me?" After all, who would better know the best people in the business than someone else in the same business?

REIA meetings are an ideal place to find referrals, sell a deal, pick up a deal, make contacts, and do almost anything else related to REO investing. As my former student Gerald Lucas says, those meetings are the water cooler that serves as a networking hot spot, social scene, and deal-making forum for this business.

> Sometimes professional and referral organizations also provide a good starting place. A few additional ones to consider include:
>
> - ServiceMagic (www.servicemagic.com). This national Colorado-based group connects consumers with screened and approved local service professionals.
> - The Blue Book Building and Construction Network (www.thebluebook.com). This national organization targets the building and construction industries.

- **Appraisers.com (www.appraisers.com).** This online advertising service helps consumers and financial institutions locate a real estate appraiser in any county in the United States.
- **MortgageLoan.com (www.mortgageloan.com).** This website includes a network of mortgage bankers, lenders, and financial professionals around the nation.

Tips to Take with You

When you are interviewing potential team members, it's not enough that someone's nice or personable. Here are a few things to consider:

- **Interview a number of different people.** Even if you think the first person you interview is a good fit, don't stop there. Interview others, too. You'll likely learn more about the business while at the same time gaining name recognition, interview expertise, and self-confidence, and you very well may find a better expert for the job.
- **Maintain control of the interview.** You should be the one who asks the questions. Being in control is one more way you establish your credibility.
- **Always be professional.** Professionalism includes being polite, direct, and up front in your approach with others.
- **If you're meeting potential team members in person, dress professionally.** First impressions are lasting impressions. You have only seconds to create a good impression, so make those seconds count.
- **Ask for referrals to other professionals.** A bank will know REO agents and other potential team members. You might even pick up a direct referral to a property or a bank's REO agent.
- **Network, network, network.** Every encounter, every step—backward and forward—is an opportunity to learn and to network.
- **When it comes to certain professionals like an accountant, one is enough.** But when you're looking for a mortgage lender or an REO agent, more is better.

- **Follow up with each contact you make.** That means a thank-you via e-mail. Whether you end up with the person on your professional team or not, it's another opportunity to show your professionalism, gain name recognition, and lay the groundwork for possible deals over the long term.
- **In some situations, you may want to offer a finder's fee if someone refers a deal your way.** A lucrative deal is worth the few hundred dollars, and a little appreciation can go a long way toward building important relationships.

Licensing

Make sure that all potential members of your power team, whether individuals or companies, are licensed in their field of expertise. Over the years, I've run into many people who are very nice and come across as quite knowledgeable, but they're not licensed. Whatever professional you deal with—even a termite inspection company—must be licensed. You're not trying to circumvent the law; you're complying with it. If you hire a roofer who isn't licensed, for instance, you're asking for problems. More often than not, the code enforcement inspector will drive by the property while the roofing is in progress. You could end up footing the bill for fines plus the roof replacement, then tearing off the new roof and replacing it again.

If a professional is involved in manual labor—property rehab, for example—make sure he or she is bonded and insured to protect yourself and your business in the event of an on-the-job injury.

Investor-Friendly

"Investor-friendly" isn't a buzz phrase; it's a necessity when it comes to finding the right members of your power team. No matter their business expertise, your team members need to know and understand the nuances of real estate investing.

Often you won't discover that someone is unfamiliar with investors and REOs until well into the purchase process. At best, you may end up scrambling to save a deal; at worst, the deal may fall through completely. I once worked (briefly) with an escrow company—we'll call it Company A—that had solicited my business. We were close to sealing the deal when right before the closing I discovered that Company A didn't know what it was doing. The deal turned into a big mess, and I had to get another escrow company to walk Company A through the process to salvage the deal.

Some escrow and title companies don't fully understand wholesale transactions; in particular, they may not understand those involving transactional funding (when the wholesaler uses someone else's funds for a short period of time to make the deal, and in that time flips the property to another investor). Transactional funding is a legal approach that is used often in short sales and REO transactions. Many companies, however, are suspicious of it and often are unwilling to get involved in those deals.

Always discuss your escrow and title needs up front to make sure your team members understand and are willing to work with you to meet your needs. Investors work differently from retail buyers. Your team needs to understand the difference and facilitate your efforts.

Fortunately, more and more businesses are becoming investor-friendly today. That's because investors continue to account for a big percentage of home purchases. In January 2011, for example, nearly one in four (23 percent) of existing home purchases were made by investors, according to data from the National Association of Realtors (www.realtor.org/press_room/news_releases/2011/02/january_above). That figure represented a 20 percent increase since December 2010. The significant percentage of investor purchases shows how important investors are to a real estate recovery in this country.

Experience in Working with REO Deals

REO transactions differ from many other real estate deals and often require different skills to achieve a successful closing. Your team members need experience or at the very least strong knowledge about the REO business and the creative ways in which its deals are structured.

Depending on the exit strategy, an REO investor could, for example, do a back-to-back closing, close a deal and take title in a land trust and assign their beneficial interest in that land trust to someone else at closing, or take title in a corporation. There are any number of options (we address these and other options later).

Willingness to Put Your Business First

Your power team members must be willing to put your business needs first. That seems like a tall order when you're a beginning REO investor. But if you're a serious investor with plans to bring a company repeat business, it definitely can pay for someone to be responsive to your needs. In the beginning, members of your power team should be open to the idea. It's up to you to believe in your potential and to market that potential.

If you're successful, pay on time, and make a point of being easy to work with, professionals and companies will learn to put your needs first as you build relationships with them.

Willingness to Charge Wholesale Prices

As an investor representing serious repeat business, you should expect a company to give you investor-friendly wholesale pricing. When you hire a handyman or contractor, for example, you shouldn't end up paying the going rate of $2 a square foot to paint a house. You should receive discounts with title and escrow companies, too.

Be careful, though, that you're fair in the pricing you demand. You'll have to study individual markets to find out the best rates, keeping in mind that if you pay peanuts, you get monkeys. In other words, don't go to a work center to pick up a few day laborers, then head to the nearest home improvement store for paint, drop off the workers at your property, and tell them to rehab it. I've seen people do really shabby rehabs, and the property just doesn't stack up to the competition. As a result, the property may languish on the market for months or never sell. Had the repairs been done properly, the property would have sold quickly.

Any work done on your property should be done well and at a reasonable price. It's not necessary to hire contractors. But do hire rehabbers—individuals who understand the business and know how to manage an entire project so it's done right.

Professional Appearance and Operations

Your team members, even though they're your equals and not your employees, represent you in your transactions. They should be professional in appearance and demeanor, and knowledgeable in their fields. Your credibility and integrity are at stake. The more carefully you choose your power team in the beginning, the fewer headaches you'll have later on.

Chapter 8

WHERE TO FIND THE BEST REOs IN YOUR MARKET

Doing your homework makes identifying the right REOs easier.
                                                    —Jeff Adams

As a beginning REO investor who has set your goals, identified and studied your target market, found your financing, and put together much of your power team, you now must find those pennies-on-the-dollar REO deals that are at the heart of your business. As I've discussed, finding those deals takes focus and diligence, and you'll have to be ready to move quickly should a deal come up, but the rewards are well worth the effort.

WHAT TO LOOK FOR IN A POTENTIAL DEAL

As you begin looking for potential REO deals, price obviously matters. But a few other not-so-obvious essentials to keep in mind include:

- Your target market—the geographic area where you plan to buy houses.
- The type of property you've chosen for your focus—whether single-family or multifamily, starter home, or dream home.
- Your exit strategy—how you expect to make a profit, whether you plan to buy and wholesale, buy and flip retail, or rent for long-term income.
- Your professional and thorough approach to deals—what will differentiate you from much of your competition.

No matter how well-priced a property is, if it doesn't dovetail with your exit strategies, leave it and move on. Also be careful if a property is located next to a freeway, busy intersection, or under power lines—all can severely curtail the property's potential to flip quickly or rent. If you find a hot deal on a palatial home, leave it, too, unless you absolutely, unequivocally already have a firm buyer. Your profits on any deal come after you sell or rent the property—

again, following through with your exit strategy. High-end properties are a tough market. First-time homebuyers, low-income buyers
and renters, and singles and young married couples are much easier to attract as buyers and renters, and the properties they look for
in general are much less expensive—to buy, to maintain, and to
market.

As a beginning REO investor, the properties to look for include:

- Those that are considerably underpriced when compared with
  other listings in the area.
- Those that can be purchased in as-is condition.
- Those new to the market.
- Those on the market more than 90 days.
- Those that have had a revision to the list price (a price drop).

THE MULTIPLE LISTING SERVICE (MLS)

Your quest for the best deals starts with the local Multiple Listing Service (MLS). Nationwide, with nearly 107 million home listings and
more than 3.3 million property listings, the MLS represents the most
comprehensive and complete property-for-sale searchable database
available today. It is also the most commonly used vehicle for liquidat-
ing real estate. The majority of REO properties today are sold through
the MLS. It's not the only place to find REO deals, but it's a good
place to start.

Other online sources for REOs include national websites like Redfin (www.redfin.com), HomeFinder (www.homefinder.com), back-
page.com (www.backpage.com), and HomeGain (www.homegain.
com), as well as other local, regional, and subscription-only sites. However, listings from some of these sites often aren't as up-to-date as the
MLS—they can be a week or more behind, not as comprehensive, or
not as quick and easy to use. All of these factors can and do mean the
difference between finding and making a great deal, and having to
settle for a mediocre deal or none at all.

Details to Know

Up-to-date listings and quick responses to the listings as soon as they appear on the MLS—first day out—are crucial in the REO investing business. In the REO investing business, the old saying "The early bird catches the worm" is advice to follow diligently.

Property listings can change every day. New listings can appear, old listings can drop off, and old listings that have dropped off can reappear. If a property no longer appears on the MLS, that doesn't necessarily mean you've lost out on a deal. When an offer on a property is accepted, not all the conditions of sale may be met—funding could fall through, for example—and the property could end up relisted on the MLS. That's why it's critical to continue to follow up on a property until it sells.

The Information in Each Listing

The MLS provides a comprehensive, searchable snapshot of properties for sale in an area. Information on a property can include:

- Location, including county, city, subdivision, lot, address.
- Size of house in square feet, and room dimensions.
- Any special features in the home.
- Garage or carport, if any.
- Listing price of property.
- Short sale or revision of list price (price reduction, and date and amount of cut).
- Property taxes or assessed value of property.
- Year built.
- Date listed and number of days on the MLS.
- Photos—exterior and interior—of the property.
- Permits (building permits pulled for the property, a new roof, or an aftermarket addition, for example).
- Property status (active, pending).

Some Multiple Listing Services (depending on the region, state, or city) offer an added feature that allows a user to create a map with virtual stick pins showing properties by location and price. It's a great tool when determining prices of comparable properties in an area. Remember the map of your target market that you picked up earlier in order to build your own on-the-wall database? This is an online version that can be of great help in showing market trends and locations of the trends.

Price Reductions

Pay attention to price reductions on REO properties—as mentioned earlier, they're called "revision to list price," "price drop," or "price reduction"; they can save you thousands of dollars on the right property. Most MLS listings will also state the amount of the revision and the date it occurred. Your competitors often fail to notice these price changes simply because they're not looking for them.

A price reduction can signify that a bank is highly motivated to get rid of the property quickly. The bank may have held the property for a long time, or there could be some problems with the property. It's important to do your due diligence to make sure that any problems with the property aren't insurmountable or won't translate into a bottomless pit when it comes to repair costs.

The properties with revisions to the list price won't show up in the MLS's new listings, so it's necessary to go back to the MLS's search tool and modify your search by "revision to list price," "price reduction," or "price drop."

How to Get Access to the MLS

Several options are available to access the up-to-date MLS, beyond going to the time, trouble, and expense of getting your own real estate license. Most of the options begin with finding a real estate agent who will work with you. Whatever the option, though, they all can be win-win situations for the various parties involved.

Friends and Family

If you have friends or family members who are Realtors, contact them and ask if they would be willing to send you the MLS's daily list of properties. In exchange, have them make your offers to banks for potential REO deals. Realtors are paid on commission, so if a bank accepts your offer on an REO and the deal closes, the Realtor's reward is the commission. After a few weeks and successful deals, go back to the Realtor and ask him or her to give you direct access to the MLS. In return, you will continue to let that Realtor write your offers and do your deals—more and regular commissions for the Realtor, and more deals for you.

Realtor Assistant

Another approach to gain MLS access involves asking your Realtor friends or family members to designate you as their assistant so that you then will have MLS access. You'll need to be registered with the local Board of Realtors to do that.

New Agent

Alternatively, contact a local real estate brokerage—some of the big national firms are Century 21, ReMax, Tarbell Realtors, and Keller Williams Realty—and ask if it has any new agents. The more seasoned agents already have clientele and aren't usually interested in writing a lot of lowball offers on REO properties. (The best approach to REO buying involves making an offer on every single good property that meets your criteria in your target market, and doing it on the first day the property is listed.) New agents generally will work harder to find a deal, are more willing to take direction, and will invest more time monitoring the market.

Once you identify one or more agents, meet with them, and ask if they would be willing to write offers for you as an investor. Be sure to point out that as an investor, you will bring them many deals regularly if they are willing to work with you. Your goal is to educate agents on the premise that working with you as an investor can be well worth their while financially. Among the advantages of working with you:

- Time efficiency. The agent won't have to spend time driving you around town to show you properties. You will preview the properties on your own.

- Fast commissions. Investors buy multiple properties in a year.
- Stable base of income. Investors can create a secure and stable income—a comfort level—for an agent.

Google

Still another approach to MLS access is to Google "real estate agent" and your city to find agents in your market. Then contact those agents and describe the offer/opportunity mentioned earlier.

ZipRealty

If meeting a real estate agent face-to-face isn't important to you, you might try to find an agent through ZipRealty (www.ziprealty.com). This site has agents who can work with you in your market. The agents in turn will give you as an investor access to the MLS in your market and then write your offers. It's very efficient.

Alternative to Direct MLS Access

If you don't have direct MLS access through an agent or Realtor, it's possible to log on to the National Association of Realtors' website (www.realtor.com) and search its property listings database. The available listings aren't as up-to-date as the MLS. In fact, they are generally three to seven days behind it. But the database can be a good starting point for your REO search.

HOW TO READ THE MLS

Remember the early-bird approach? As an investor, you must check the MLS daily or open your inbox daily and review the MLS listings sent to you by your agent (on your power team) or an REO agent with whom you have a relationship (more on REO agents in Chapter 9). Search the various entries—using either the MLS search tool or another tool you have available—by pertinent keywords that meet your criteria. For example, use words like "REO," "bank-owned," and "fixer-upper." If you find a potential deal, study the listing more closely. It contains a wealth of information that usually will simplify culling your choices.

DISSECTING AN MLS LISTING

Here is a selection of information from an MLS listing, along with an interpretation of what it all means.

Property A
Location: 123 Main Street, Anywhere, USA
Price: $95,000
Status: Active
Size: 1,200 square feet
Year Built: 1957
Permits: roofing, new addition
Bedrooms: 3
Baths: 2
Other: Family/dining room, utility room
Amenities: Brick patio, 2-car attached garage, backyard fenced (chain link)
Days Listed: 1
Lot Size: 80 by 137 [10,960 square feet, or about ¼ acre]
Agent: ID 12345 A. B. Broker
Prop. Taxes: $1,000

Analysis: On paper, the property appears to be a desirable property to buy and flip to a retail buyer, probably a first-time homebuyer. Positive aspects include its price (well below comparable properties in the area), location, and size, as well as the spacious lot. It also has an attached two-car garage, which is a big selling feature in terms of resale value. The extra bedroom, indoor utility room, and fenced backyard also make it great for small children. Other after-repair houses in the area tend to be selling in the $130,000 range. In photos, it appears that the house needs some minor cosmetic repair and kitchen appliances.

Bonus: This listing gives me the User ID number and name of the broker. By taking that information and inputting it into the MLS search tool at the bottom of the listing page, I can see everything that broker has on the market right now and possibly find other properties that might be potential deals. Also, by checking what else he has on the market, when I call him I can talk about his other properties, too. That conveys I'm a serious investor, not a looky loo.

Conclusion: We will make an offer on the property

DISSECTING AN MLS LISTING II

Property B
Location: 123 Your Street, Anywhere, USA
Price: $74,000
Status: Active
Size: 1900 square feet
Year Built: 1972
Permits: None
Bedrooms: 3
Baths: 2
Other: Living/dining room w/built-ins
Amenities: Tile flooring throughout.
Days Listed: 97
Lot Size: 7,530 square feet
Agent: ID 22222 C. Broker
Prop. Taxes: $1,635
Comments: Bank-owned

Analysis: Property is a good size in a solid location, popular with first-time homebuyers. Comparable after-repair value (ARV) prices are in the $120,000 to $130,000 range. Photos of the property show it has nice curb appeal—

leaded glass front door, nice porch. The deal possibly fell through several times because it's been on the market so long (possibly a motivated seller). The interior tile floor is a plus (easy maintenance), but the checkered floor in the kitchen has to go. Kitchen will need a complete makeover. Exterior photo of rear shows what looks like a possible illegal modification (no permit listed on MLS). I'll need to find out if there really is a permit, and if not, the seriousness of the violation before deciding whether to make offer on the home. This listing says the property is a three-bedroom, two-bath. A quick call to my title company and I find out the title says it's a three-bedroom, one-bath.

Bonus: Since the property has been on the market a long time and deals on it likely fell through several times, the seller likely is motivated to get rid of the property. This could be a situation to make a lowball offer—perhaps $45,000—since it will cost so much to repair and bring up to code. But before making the offer, call the agent to discuss the property, be aboveboard, discuss the situation, and ask how low an offer the bank will accept. Don't call on every offer, but do call if you're very serious about the property. Again, it's about the agent recognizing you're a serious investor.

Conclusion: We will ask the listing agent if he will make an offer for us.

New Listings

Look for all the new listings described as "active" as opposed to "pending." The latter are properties on which an offer has been accepted and the sale is pending. Are any of the listings in your target area? If they're not in your predetermined geographic area, move on for the time being. Focus is essential to early success. Do any of the listings fit your target market? For example, does a property make sense to wholesale to another investor, to repair and sell at retail to a first-time homebuyer, or to rehab and hold as a rental for regular income?

House Size

How big is a property? How many square feet? How many bedrooms and baths? A three-bedroom, two-bath home has more appeal to buyers and renters than a three-bedroom, one-bath home, and a three-bedroom, one-bath home has more potential than a two-bedroom, one-bath home.

Pay attention to the lot size, too. Often bigger is better, but too big isn't necessarily a choice property. Here's where common sense, comparable properties, and gut feeling come into play. If there's absolutely no way you would ever under any circumstances live in a particular home, don't buy that property!

Construction Date

When was a property built? The MLS listing will tell you the year of construction. The date matters because likely some of the better REO deals may be on older homes. They're also prime properties for first-time homebuyers. Conversely, though, many first-time homebuyers like the amenities and extras that often come with newer homes.

Consider all the aspects of each property to determine your best deal. Pay close attention to whether the property has strong resale or rental potential, because it doesn't mean much to buy a property at a great price if you don't have a ready buyer or renter.

Be careful, however, of the much older homes. They can come with big repair expenses and complications involving things like asbestos, which require special handling and removal.

Photos

MLS listings generally include interior and exterior photos of a property and the lot. Look closely; the words in the listing may tell one story while the photos tell another. A property could be in very poor condition, for example, or have a new tile roof that can be attractive to first-time homebuyers.

A kitchen or other part of a house could need a dramatic and expensive remodel, or there could be water leaks. Either might be indicated by the pictures, but not by the wording in the listing.

Pictures also indicate positive (and negative) selling points like a garage, outside (and sometimes teardown) structures, interior laundry, illegal additions, and more. Do not, however, rely on photos to paint the entire picture. It's essential to inspect the property, too.

Days on Market

Often the newest listings offer you top opportunities to snag great deals. But don't underestimate potential deals on properties that have been on the market a long time—60 to 90 or more days. These may provide an opportunity to make a lowball offer on a solid property that requires only minor cosmetic upgrades. Such a property can be a good deal as long as it doesn't have major problems.

If a property has languished on the market, hasn't sold, is in the right neighborhood (you should know that from researching your target market), and meets your target criteria, find out more about it. Contact the listing agent named on the MLS listing for more information about the property. Check if the electric meter has been pulled. If so, it indicates building code violations. Find out what the violations are. Also visually inspect the property. This could be the right deal so that with some minor repair, the property could make an excellent and profitable flip or rental.

Location

Everyone knows that location, location, location counts with real estate. When it comes to finding REO deals, the adage is no exception. No matter how good the numbers are, no matter how closely the property is in line with your exit strategies, if it's in a bad location, forget it and move on.

Obviously, you—or your real estate agent—can't physically see every property on the MLS. But once you've narrowed the list of potential properties, locate the property on Google Maps (www. google.com/maps). Zoom in to see if there are any obvious location issues like power lines or busy streets. Eliminate those from your list.

Then, after you've narrowed your list further, you should visually inspect the remaining properties. To make the process easier, I use mapping software like Microsoft Streets & Trips (www.microsoft.com/streets/911/Products.aspx). I simply plug in the addresses of the list of properties I need to review, and the software gives me turn-by-turn instructions on how to get to each one efficiently and quickly.

One day recently I was checking the new MLS listings and came across what sounded like a great property in my target market, San Bernardino, California. The price was right, and it was a good property to flip. But it was located on Eleventh Street near a major freeway, so I passed on the deal. As a general rule, a home located close to a busy highway doesn't have good resale value.

RED FLAG WARNING

If homes near power lines don't usually sell well, forget them when it comes to REO investing. Exceptions to rules exist, but as an REO investor, you should seek out deals that can be picked up for pennies on the dollar, then flipped quickly for profits with a minimum amount of cash and effort. You should not concentrate your efforts on what might be an exception to a general rule or trend.

Pending Sales

An often overlooked source of good REO deals are those properties listed as "pending" on the MLS. These are properties on which an offer has been received and accepted, and the deal is in the process of being finalized. If those properties meet your investment criteria and remain pending on the MLS for a couple of months or more, contact the listing agent. He or she may be having trouble with the buyer meeting all the terms of the contract.

Introduce yourself to the agent as a cash buyer. A sample conversation:

My name is John Doe. I'm a cash buyer and saw that your property at 123 Main Street has been pending a long time.

What's going on? If you're having problems getting the deal closed, please let me know if the deal falls through. I'm interested in the property.

The best way for a real estate agent to look good in the eyes of the property owner, in this case a bank, is to have a backup offer in case a deal falls through. An added bonus of talking to agents in situations like this is that it helps you build relationships with them. And relationships can lead to your goal of having agents bring you the best deals first.

MORE OPTIONS FOR FINDING PROPERTIES

The MLS should play a big role in your search for REO properties, but it's only one aspect of what should become your regular routine when searching for opportunities. To be first in line for the best REO deals requires a multifaceted approach.

Beyond the MLS

One source for deals isn't enough, just as one broker or one lender or one banker isn't enough to ensure you can move immediately on the right deal. Check the Internet for the keywords "bank-owned" and "REO," then follow the links. If a property comes on the market that's a steal of a deal—and you have run the numbers and gone to see the property, too—then drop everything, visit the agent offering the property, and have him or her write the offer for you immediately. Those agents you speak with need to know that you are an all-cash buyer who can make a deal quickly and cleanly. That's why, after all, they will come back to you again and again. It makes their job of selling a property much easier.

Websites

Plenty of websites also have searchable property database listings. Some are easier to use than others—and, again, most may not have listings as current as those on the MLS—but they're all a starting point and a way to discover what's going on in various markets.

A few websites with searchable property listings include Realtor. com (www.realtor.com), Redfin (www.redfin.com), HomeGain (www. homegain.com), and HomeFinder (www.homefinder.com). For local websites, Google "real estate," "for sale," and "listings" along with your targeted area.

Other Professionals

It's essential to develop relationships with REO agents who can bring you the deals. We talk more about that in a later chapter. Other sources of deals include those professionals you count as part of your power team, and even those you don't. Every encounter is a potential source of a deal. Let members of your team know you're always open to great deals. When you approach lenders, bankers, brokers, lawyers, agents, or title companies about a potential deal, don't walk away without handing them your card and asking if they know of someone else who can help you or if they know of any other deal that might interest you.

Always leave the door open for other deals. Here are two sample statements that do just that:

- "If the deal with your other investor falls through, here's my card; don't hesitate to call me. I do all-cash deals and can close quickly and efficiently. I also would like to bring you additional business on a regular basis."
- "Do you know of any similar deals that might interest me? I'm an investor who does all-cash deals and can close quickly and efficiently. I also would like to do business with you on a regular basis."

Small Banks and Credit Unions

Small banks and credit unions generally don't have huge portfolios of REOs, but often they're motivated sellers because they are less able to afford the nonperforming assets these repossessed properties represent.

Get to know the REO representatives at your local banks and credit unions, and let them know you're an investor who can pay cash and close quickly.

The federal government over the past two years has been careful to assist larger national banks to maintain their financial strength. But many of the smaller banks and credit unions, especially in the Sunbelt states, have been heavily impacted by the recession and left to survive or fail under the weight of bad loans.

Astute REO investors should find these imperiled financial institutions in their areas and contact their REO staff. Try to meet in person with these individuals and offer to assist them by buying their REO inventory. Work at building a relationship with the asset managers who are the decision makers, and follow up with them periodically to see if they have any new inventory coming on the market.

Bird Dogs and More

Bird dogs can be another source of deals. "Bird dog" is the slang name given to people like meter readers and others who bring you leads to often vacant or run-down properties, generally in exchange for a finder's fee. If a deal nets you $5,000, the $500 fee is well worth the expense. In fact, if word gets out that you are willing to pay sizable finder's fees for properties, watch what happens to your business. Of course, pay attention to state laws related to such fees. Obviously it's not legal to pay an agent a side fee other than his or her commission.

Look Around

When you're driving to see potential deals in a neighborhood, also watch for REOs that haven't yet been listed on the MLS. They're usually very noticeable—a dead lawn, trash in the yard, possibly mail piled on the doorstep, and sometimes a lockbox on the door. A "For Sale" sign may or may not be up on the property. Better yet, use bird dogs to bring these deals to you for a small fee—even $10 or $20—and ask for pictures!

After a bank repossesses a property, it usually takes the agent about 30 days to get the house on the market—the house has to be cleaned out, locks have to be changed, utilities have to be turned on, and so forth. As an investor, if you find a house pre-MLS listing, contact the listing agent. Typically look for a sign or a piece of paper taped in one of the windows of the vacant property that gives a name and phone number in case of emergency or for information.

Call the agent and tell him or her that you're interested in the property. Will the agent write the offer for you right now? If the answer is "No, not until the property is listed," ask if the agent will take your offer now and submit it to the bank as soon as the property is listed formally. Often this can be an easy way to put in that all-important first offer.

HUD AND VA PROPERTIES

The Federal Housing Administration (FHA) has insured more than 37 million mortgages across the country since 1934. When one of its properties goes through foreclosure and isn't sold, it ends up repossessed by the U.S. Department of Housing and Urban Development (HUD). HUD in turn must liquidate these properties.

HUD first offers the properties to owner-occupants and nonprofit organizations. But if the properties aren't sold, the homes are made available to the public, including investors. Properties are sold as is, and they usually fetch slightly below-market prices. The properties often need substantial repairs, but occasionally an investor can find great properties at great prices. To get an idea of what's available, check out the HUD Homes website (http://hudhomestore.com/HudHome/Index.aspx).

If as an investor, you're interested in REOs held by HUD, keep a few things in mind, including:

- Because HUD homes typically are less expensive than other homes, they often can be more appealing to low- and moderate-income buyers. If your exit strategy targets this market, you may want to consider HUD homes.

- Watch for HUD homes that have been on the market a long time as well as those in which deals have fallen through. They can be excellent buys.
- Only real estate agents who have registered with HUD can present offers on HUD properties.
- Winning bids on HUD properties typically are those that give HUD the most net funds. A good strategy calls for getting a solid HUD broker on your team who may be willing to take a slightly reduced commission at the front end along with the possibility of a commission at the other end of the transaction, when you sell the property. Another strategy calls for finding a broker who will take a flat-fee commission of $500 to submit offers on your behalf.

The U.S. Department of Veterans Affairs (VA) also issues and guarantees home loans nationwide to qualifying veterans. Like HUD, the VA also ends up with REOs after foreclosure and has to liquidate them. For more information, check out the page on the VA website dealing with home loans (http://www.benefits.va.gov/homeloans/).

THE IMPORTANCE OF YOUR REAL ESTATE AGENT

Your real estate agent is a key member of your power team. In addition to providing you access to the MLS, the agent should know the type of deals you're looking for. He or she also should be ready to move when a potential deal comes up. To do that, make sure the agent:

- Sends you new REO lists daily.
- Submits your offers immediately, not only to increase their chances of acceptance but also to hinder the competition.
- Follows up on the offers you make until the properties are sold.
- States specific terms with every submitted offer. Those terms, which we'll talk more about later, include:
  - All-cash transaction.
  - As-is condition.
  - Quick closing.

- No contingencies.
- Verification of cash or proof of funds.

Don't forget that, in large part, your success depends on writing offers on every REO property the first day it comes on the market.

FOLLOW UP TO NET RESULTS

No matter the source of a potential REO deal or how many offers you or your agent submit, always follow up until the property sale is final. Follow up, follow up, and follow up. If I'm interested in a property, and my offer isn't accepted, I contact the listing agent every two weeks until the property is sold.

Sometimes property sales fall through when some aspect of the sales contract is not fulfilled. A buyer—especially a first-time home-buyer—might not get financing, or the contract from an investor was based on a contingency that wasn't met. If you've remained in contact with the listing agent and followed up on the property as suggested, you may get a call from the listing agent informing you that the property sale has fallen through: "Are you still interested?" Bingo—you get another shot at the property. Simply ask the REO agent to re-present your offer to the bank. That also saves the listing agent the hassle of relisting the property for sale.

I recently purchased a property that I initially had made an unsuccessful offer on three months earlier. The property had fallen out of escrow, and the listing agent called, wanting to know if I would be willing to pay a bit more for the property. I was, and did, and walked away with a stellar REO deal.

Chapter 9

THE IMPORTANCE OF REO AGENTS: FINDING THE BEST AND GETTING THEM ON YOUR SIDE

I offer on every single suitable property that comes on the market in my area.

—Jeff Adams

When it comes to getting the best deals on most products, people are warned to avoid the middleman. That caveat definitely doesn't apply in the REO investing business. In the REO business, it's the middleman—the REO agent—who can make your life easier and the deals sweeter.

REO agents or brokers are one of the best resources available to help REO investors build their businesses. Developing and nurturing contacts with these agents will dramatically increase your chances for success.

WHO ARE REO AGENTS?

Banks hire REO agents to sell the repossessed properties in their portfolios. These specialists are brought in because banks need to get rid of the properties and don't want the hassle of working individually with buyers, many of whom are novices.

REO agents know their markets—and your target markets. Most have been in the industry for several years and are top performers. As a group, they wield considerable control over the existing REO inventory. Building and maintaining relationships with these agents not only can give you the inside track on REO inventory but also can net other real estate investment opportunities, including wholesale deals, connections to top agents, and valuable information about your competition. REO agents have properties to move and are ready and willing to work with buyers who know how to do the deals quickly and efficiently.

Why Bother?

In case you question whether nurturing yet another relationship is worth the time and effort, keep in mind that your goal as an REO investor is to have the deals come to you. That will happen if you get to know the specialists known as REO agents and show them that you deliver as promised. That means offering an agent an easy outlet for successive all-cash deals with fast closings, few complications, and minimal work.

Your goal, as mentioned earlier, is to become an agent's "pocket buyer," the first investor he or she turns to with the best deals, and sometimes before they appear on the MLS. Most successful REO investors—myself and my associates included—will tell you their REO agents routinely come to them with the hottest deals. In exchange, though, you have to be ready to act on a potential deal. I might get a call from an agent at 8:00 p.m. on a Friday night about a property selling for $120,000 that's worth $180,000. I'll drop every-thing and go right out to look at it so that I can promptly make an offer or not. You must be willing to do the same.

Big Rewards

Depending on the relationship you have with them, some REO agents will bring you deals before they're made public.

An REO agent can help make your deals smooth and speedy, too; using one can help you avoid spending months trying to get a deal done on your own. Be careful not to be greedy with your pricing and approach. Be fair so that both the agent and his or her employer—the bank—are satisfied, and you'll still walk away with handsome profits and often the potential that your REO agent will bring you future deals.

Consider the central Florida investor and real estate agent Alex Galitsky. He finds many deals for other investors and earns a commis-sion of only $1,000 to $5,000 per deal. But all each deal requires from him is a *few minutes'* work. Galitsky makes up for the smaller commis-sions with the sheer volume of his deals. (Galitsky also buys properties to rehab and flip for profits—$20,000 to $60,000 per property—and keeps other properties as rentals for their cash flow and long-term appreciation.)

What an REO Agent Expects from You

REO agents don't want to waste their time with looky-loo investors. They want serious buyers who close deals with minimal work. No one—including you as an investor—gets paid until a deal is complete. Agents certainly don't get paid to give out information. They're busy, and as an investor you need to be aware of that and respect their time. Do your homework before you contact an agent.

As I mentioned above, to nab the best deals and the best REO agents, always be ready to go when presented with a new prospect. Some other essentials that REO agents like to see in investors:

- A willingness to close quickly.
- Verifiable proof of funds (submitted with an offer).
- A professional approach and appearance.
- Knowledge of the market.
- Politeness and respect.
- A willingness to do the legwork and homework.
- Follow-through.
- A willingness to close on deal after deal.

REO agents don't like blind offers from investors who obviously haven't done their homework, who make ridiculous lowball offers, and who don't bother to include proof that they can do the deal (proof of funds, which we'll talk about later).

If an agent has to ask you for data and you don't bother to send it, your credibility as an investor goes in the trash along with your offer.

How to Find an REO Agent

Many of the sources that helped you find a real estate agent for your power team can help in your search for REO agents. Use one real estate agent as a referral to find others. Banks, title companies, lenders, contractors, and more also can help direct you to the players—big and small—in the REO market. Talk to other investors as well as to members of Real Estate Investor Association (REIA) clubs. Check out, among others, the National Association of Realtors (www.realtor.com), Zillow (www.zillow.com), HomeGain (www.homegain.com); the U.S. Department of Housing and Urban Development (www.hud.gov), and Redfin (www.redfin.com).

Whale Agents as Sources for Deals

The term *whale agent* refers to a volume seller who controls many of the properties in a given area. A whale agent may be the primary REO agent for a bank and a big seller around town. To find who the whales are, ask other investors, banks, and professionals about who controls most of the properties for sale, and drive the neighborhood to see which agent has the most signs out.

After you identify the whales, check their listings on the MLS (you can search the MLS by the agent's name or identification number). Study their listings so that when you speak with them, you know about their listings and can talk about them. Whether or not you're interested in a specific property, you can set yourself apart as a serious buyer and not just a looky loo if you can discuss the agent's properties knowledgeably.

If you're interested in one of the whale agent's properties, ask if the agent will write offers on your behalf. If not, have your regular agent— on your power team—submit an offer, then follow up to make sure the offer was received. Introduce yourself as an investor who does all-cash deals and can close quickly and easily. Point out that you made an offer on a particular property (if you did so), and then ask, "What else do you have coming on the market in the next few weeks?" If you keep following up, eventually that whale agent could come to you with deals—perhaps even before they're listed on the MLS.

HOW TO PERSUADE AN AGENT TO WORK WITH YOU

If you're just starting out, a big challenge is to get an REO agent to accept you as a serious buyer. As with other aspects of the business, that's where your professionalism, appearance, and approach can really help. Your goal is to convince the agent that you are the best and fastest all-cash closer and that you will be there and follow through every time a deal is right. Closing deals, after all, is what the bank hired the agent to do.

The Right Attitude and Approach

Carry yourself with confidence. Think about the importance of conviction and commitment as discussed earlier in the book. REO agents are in contact with many investors. Why should they consider you as their pocket buyer who gets the best deals? If you don't take your investing seriously, no one else can be expected to take you seriously, either.

Before you meet with an REO agent, study the MLS to determine not only what properties the agent is offering but also their locations, conditions, and more. Background yourself about the agent, too, by talking to others and checking out the agent on the Internet. By doing your homework on the agent and his or her properties, you demonstrate that you take the agent—and a possible relationship—seriously.

Your Appearance
Dress like a serious investor. Even if it's the middle of summer, wear a suit or a company uniform that's as simple as a polo shirt embroidered with your company's logo.

Communication—Verbal and Written
Make sure your communications, whether written or verbal, are professional. Your written correspondence—hard-copy, e-mail, or text—should be clean, with no errors or typos, and to the point.

Follow Up
After you meet with an agent, follow up and keep following up again and again. Even if an agent doesn't take you seriously at first or isn't interested in working with you, follow up and keep making offers on his or her properties. Eventually, agents will realize that you are a serious investor and will take your offers seriously. They may also give you

access to REOs before they're listed on the MLS. (We talk more about what it takes to close a deal in later chapters.)

Win-Win Strategy

Persuading REO agents to work with you on a regular basis as their pocket buyer who has the investment cash is largely about convincing them of the efficacy and profit—theirs and yours—in your win-win strategy. It's similar to the strategy that generally helps persuade real estate agents to work with you to provide MLS access:

- **Time efficiency.** The agent won't have to spend time driving you around town to show you properties. You simply will e-mail or fax your offers on properties that meet your criteria. When and if the offer is accepted, the all-cash closing is swift.
- **Fast commissions.** As an investor you buy multiple properties in a year. That translates to regular and steady commissions.
- **Additional income.** With you as his or her pocket buyer, the agent will have the opportunity as your pocket listing agent to earn commissions selling the properties, too.

SPELL OUT YOUR NEEDS

For your relationship with the REO agent to be successful, you as the investor must clearly define your needs.

Type of Property

The REO agent needs to know the geographic parameters of your target market and exactly the type of properties that interest you and dovetail with your exit strategy. For example, as a beginning investor with the goal of flipping a property, the following types of houses can be solid investments:

- **Houses that are easy to sell.** Typically that means three- and four-bedroom homes with at least two baths. In today's crowded market, often the price difference is minimal between a two- and three-bedroom home, but the larger homes can be much easier to sell. Some buyers these days also like newer homes with more amenities.

- **Houses investors want.** Again, the newer three- and four-bedroom homes with multiple baths can be great rental properties. Older homes with a similar number of bedrooms but only one bath may not rent as well or at as high monthly rents. Condominiums and homes in planned communities with high monthly association fees may not be as easy to sell, either.
- **Houses in need of minimal repairs.** As a new investor, major rehabs—houses in need of major interior or exterior overhauls—can be sources of bigger headaches than profits. An REO agent needs to know you're not interested in major rehabs for now. It's also easier to calculate a property's after-repair value (ARV) without having to factor in big (and possibly growing) repair expenses. If you like the idea of getting involved in major rehabs, it may be wiser to wait until you're a bit more established as an REO investor. Plenty of investors just starting out have lost tens of thousands of dollars on properties requiring major rehabs because of inexperience and unforeseen expenses.

PROPERTY PRICES

Before looking for REO properties, an investor knows the dollar amount he or she wants to and is able to spend on a property. Make sure your REO agent knows that amount, too.

RED FLAG WARNING

If a potential property is outside your dollar range, leave it and move on. Other properties will be within your range, and they will come with less risk than that inherent in overextending yourself.

The Role of an REO Agent

Keep in mind that in addition to handling offers on properties, an REO agent performs many roles for a bank, and doesn't have the time to waste dealing with a bumbling or unprepared REO investor.

Among the jobs of an agent:

- **Giving a broker price opinion (BPO).** A BPO is a comparatively fast valuation of a home, often based on comparable properties (comps), with or without a drive-by, and without going through the time and expense of a formal appraisal.
- **Doing an occupancy check.** A bank may have repossessed a property, but that doesn't always mean the property is vacant. Squatters and defiant homeowners could end up living in the property even if the locks have been changed. If a property you purchase is supposed to be vacant, the REO agent should make sure it is.
- **Conducting property tax searches and more.** Agents should be able to provide reports and data associated with a property.
- **Arranging winterization.** In the fall or winter, for example, the agent makes sure a property is secure against the elements.
- **Re-key properties.** When a bank repossesses a property, the agent arranges to have the home secured by changing locks.
- **Maintain and manage a property.** That includes making sure the property is cleaned up, needed repairs completed, and utilities and more handled properly.

Chapter 10

BUYING REO PROPERTIES AT AUCTION

Pay attention to who is buying at auctions. They're not just the competition. They're your potential buyers, too.

—Jeff Adams

With a glut of foreclosures and REO properties on the market today—and a looming shadow inventory of recent and pending foreclosures not yet on the market—many banks look to alternative methods to dispose of their REOs. Those alternatives include auctions and real estate disposition companies, which can be great sources of REO deals as long as you know what you're doing and how to play the game.

WIN-WIN SITUATION

AUCTION GLOSSARY

Absolute auction: An auction in which properties are sold for the highest bid, with no minimum bids established, regardless of price.

As is: Without modification. Most properties at auction are sold in their current condition; it's the buyer's responsibility to examine the property.

Bank letter of credit: A letter from a bank certifying that a person is worthy of a given level of credit; the same as a proof-of-funds letter required with an REO offer.

Bid assistants: Employees of the auctioneer who are usually positioned throughout the crowd of bidders on the auction floor to help the auctioneer spot bidders and to help control and influence the crowd.

Bidding limit: The theoretical top price bidders will pay for a property; the limit is self-imposed and set in a bidder's mind.

Buyer's premium: A percentage amount added to the winning bid to be paid by the buyer for the services of the auctioneer.

Buyback: An item withdrawn from sale because it does not attract the reserve established by the seller.

Conditions of sale: The legal terms that govern the conduct of the sale, including acceptable methods of payment, terms, buyer's premium, and reserve prices.

Phantom bid: A nonexistent bid acknowledged by the auctioneer to create the illusion of a bid and to encourage other bidders to raise their bids.

Puffing: A price-enhancing technique that may originate with someone employed by the seller to raise the price on a property with fictitious bids.

Reserve: The minimum price that a seller is willing to accept for a property sold at auction; if a sale is subject to a reserve, it's subject to the seller's approval.

Shill: An employee of the auction company who bids against legitimate bidders to run up the price.

Tie bids: The result when two buyers bid the same price at the same time. Usually the auctioneer accepts the one he or she recognized first as the new highest bidder.

Auctions offer REO investors the opportunity to acquire properties, often at substantial discounts, while allowing lenders to liquidate a number of properties quickly. Additionally, an investor can "buy" a property at auction with minimal cash down and then quickly flip the property to someone else wholesale. Typically all it takes to hold a winning-bid property for a short time is "earnest money," usually in the form of a certified check (the amount varies depending on the terms and conditions of each auction). The earnest money is required as a deposit the day of the auction, along with a letter of credit stating you're good for the remainder of the money. The five steps to the auction acquisition and wholesale flip include:

1. Locate the property.
2. Prescreen and evaluate the property.
3. Put together and present your offer. (At an auction, that's your bid along with the earnest money in the form, usually, of a certified check in the amount required by a particular auction on the day of the auction.)
4. Find your cash buyer (to whom you will wholesale the property).
5. Close the deal and cash your profit check.

Arizona-based Dana Van Hoose has done approximately 100 deals at auction and not used his own money. In December 2010 alone, he bought three properties at auction and already had the buyers lined up for all three. His involvement was simply a matter of finalizing the deals and immediately flipping the properties to investors.

Remember Chris McLaughlin, the Florida investor with more than 100 properties held as rentals? He capitalized on the auction approach to buy many of those properties at steep discounts. He'll hold them for monthly positive cash flow income, and when prices soar again—and they will—he'll sell them off for big profits.

Types of Auctions

Most auctions are *seller reserve* auctions in which the lender/seller sets a minimum price in order for a property to sell. That minimum usually is not stated by the auctioneer.

If an auction is *absolute*, in which a minimum bid is not mandatory, be careful. This is the riskiest type of auction but can net good deals if, ahead of time, you check out the properties that interest you. If no one else is bidding on the property and the price really does seem too good to be true, the property just might have a fatal flaw. The only way to know is if you have checked it out before the auction.

A Note of Caution

As a beginning REO investor, don't be swayed by all the auction hype. Not all properties for sale at auctions are bargains, period. In fact, at some auctions properties may end up selling for well more than they would bring on the open market.

RED FLAG WARNING

Don't be sidetracked by all the auction hype. Not every property is a great deal.

So-called good auctions are typically well advertised and well staffed—though not always. Auctioneers and auction companies usually offer educational information prior to the auction and encourage would-be participants to find out more about the auction process. The downside of bidder education is that, as an investor, you may face more competition in the bidding, and that drives up the prices. That doesn't mean you should avoid these auctions; simply be aware of the possibility of stiff competition.

So-called bad auctions, in contrast, are often less-publicized, much smaller events with less inventory. They also can provide an astute investor with good purchase opportunities because there's likely to be less competition. But you must know what you're doing. It's always a good idea to visit several auctions as an observer before ever participating as a bidder.

WHO ARE THE AUCTION COMPANIES?

Some of the nation's largest auction companies play major roles in the nationwide effort of banks to liquidate REOs. Those auction companies include REDC (www.auction.com), Williams & Williams (www.williamsauction.com), and Hudson & Marshall (www.hudsonandmarshall.com). All three not only offer helpful information about the auction process on their websites but also allow online bidding for properties.

A number of local and regional auction companies also handle REO disposition for lenders. These companies often don't have major advertising budgets, so check out local newspapers and online sources to find these auctions.

Terms and Conditions of Real Estate Auctions

Before attending a real estate auction or bidding online, it's important to know all the terms and conditions of a particular auction. They spell out how much of an earnest money desposit you'll need to put down on a property you've won at bid, what deed restrictions there may be, and so on. In California, for example, earnest money must be in the form of cash or a certified check, while in Alabama an auctioneer will take a personal check. If you don't have the specified payment in the specified format, you're out of luck.

You can find the information you need in the printed materials available at the auction and/or at the auctioneer's website. At Hudson & Marshall's website, for example, it takes only a simple click on the various auction/state links to find out a given auction's requirements. Williams & Williams's website even has a "Build REO Portfolio" option that allows people to bid on multiple properties online. But here, as with all other auctions, beware of the small print under "Terms and Conditions." The terms can and do change for various auctions. For example, terms may call for properties to be sold with a restricted deed that prevents flipping a property within 90 days of closing and for more than 120 percent of the purchase price. In this case, so much for buying a property and quickly flipping it to a wholesale buyer. As an investor, don't get caught. Be prepared and know the terms ahead of time.

Wholesaling Auction Properties

As an investor, if your exit strategy for a property bought at auction calls for wholesaling it to another buyer, be prepared ahead of time.

If you're taking title to the property in a corporation, limited liability corporation (LLC), or land trust (we provide more details about these options later), bring the appropriate paperwork if you're the winning bidder, you are required to provide it.

If your auction bid is successful, collect your wholesale fee and earnest deposit from your buyer, transfer your interest in the corporation, land trust, or LLC to your buyer, and then cash your profit check.

Follow Up!

If you truly want to be successful as an investor, follow up with auction companies. Some property deals will fall through, and if you've followed up, the companies will give you the opportunity to purchase these properties. Often they'll also hold smaller less-publicized auctions of others properties that didn't sell at the initial auction. If you develop relationships with the companies, they'll invite you to participate.

LETTER TO AN AUCTION COMPANY*

ABC Investors

123 My Street
Anywhere, USA
800-000-0000

Dear Auction Company:
ABC Investors buys properties for cash, fixes them up, and resells them for profit. We are experienced buyers who understand the auction process and do our own research.

We know that often deals will fall out of escrow (or end up back on the market), and we can be your alternative buyer without any additional work on your part.

We also are interested in buying multiple properties. Additionally, if you have clients who need an immediate buyer prior to a scheduled auction, please let us know.

Thank you for your time. We look forward to hearing from you.

Sincerely,
[Name Here]
ABC Investors

*For a downloadable copy customizable to meet your needs, visit www.jeffadamsforms.com.

After you win a property at auction, follow up to make sure the auction company has all the information and documentation it needs to close the deal. Be sure to identify yourself by the specific auction, and your name and bidder number, and the property you're discussing by its location and property identification number, too.

If you lose a bid, don't walk away. Be sure to give the auction assistants your name and phone number so that you end up on their short list. If a deal with a winning bidder falls through—and many do—auction houses simply go down their short list, calling each person until they find a buyer. Don't be surprised if the phone rings after the auction and it's the auction company asking if you're still interested in a particular property. I've picked up plenty of good properties that way.

WHAT PROPERTIES TO BUY AT AUCTION

Apply the same criteria to a property at an auction that you would to any other potential property for purchase. A property should be in your target market, fit your profile for property acquisitions, meet your exit strategy needs, require only minor repair work, and be priced right.

Don't fall prey to the auctioneer and allow him to bully you into paying more for a property than you think it's worth or more than the bid limit you set for yourself. Don't exceed your predetermined top bid, period.

MORE AUCTION TIPS AND TRICKS

Here are a few more suggestions on how to enhance your chances for success at real estate auctions, large and small.

Online Bidding

Some auctions allow online bidding on properties prior to a live auction. If that's the case, thoroughly review the bidding process and requirements ahead of time. Then check out the auction brochure—online or on paper—for properties that meet your criteria. If you find one that is appealing, meets your market criteria, fits your exit strategies, and is fairly priced, it may be a good idea to bid on it before the live auction. Otherwise you could miss out on the property.

Some auctions are online only. Follow the same steps—learn the details, find the right properties, and place your bid. Again, do not exceed your maximum predetermined top bid.

Location, Location, Location

Where you physically sit in the auction arena is important. By sitting in the front, you can talk to the auctioneer and staff to develop a rapport before the auction. You're also in position so that the auctioneer can easily see you when you bid. An auctioneer acknowledges the first bid he sees; if he sees yours first, it may save you from having to make a higher bid on a property.

Build a Buyers' List

Auctions also can be a great place to build your buyers' list—the list of potential buyers for properties you want to sell. The bidders at auctions often are the buyers, too, and it can pay off for you to know them.

These bidders may be your competition, but they're also your potential buyers.

You may want to move to the back of the arena after the auction starts, but before any of the properties that interest you come up for bid, so that you can observe who is bidding on what. After the auction, introduce yourself to these bidders as an investor who buys properties and is always interested in potential buyers and in finding other properties to purchase. Ask:

> Are you interested in buying other properties? If so, I have several that may interest you. If not, may I contact you at a later date with other potential properties? Do you have properties you would be willing to wholesale?

Remember, success comes from networking and paying attention to every potential opportunity. Auctions are no exception. You may even want to consider attending an auction solely to build a buyers' list.

Be Polite

Smile and be polite and respectful to the auctioneer, the auction personnel, and other bidders. You'll get a better response, and these people can be of help to you not only during the auction but well after it's over. It's all part of your goal to persuade others to accept you as a serious investor and, in turn, bring the best deals to you.

Do Your Homework

Do your homework. Verify the condition and value of the properties that interest you prior to the auction. Determine your bidding limits ahead of time based on your criteria and evaluation of the properties. Ignore the hype, and stick to your predetermined maximum bids. Again (and again and again), don't overbid. If you do, you are likely to reduce your profit when you flip the property.

More Follow-up

Many properties that were presumably sold at auction actually will fall through and get reauctioned at another live or online auction shortly afterward. If you missed out on a property at the main auction, check the auction house's website a few days after the sale to verify that the particular property actually was sold and isn't back on the auction block.

Auctions aren't for the undisciplined or faint of heart. However, for those who do their homework and stick to their game plans, auctions are an ongoing opportunity to pick up REO properties and build the relationships that make great REO deals happen.

Chapter 11

THE RIGHT WAY TO EVALUATE DEALS AND PRICE A PROPERTY

A property may seem like a great deal on paper, but reality is something else entirely.

— **Jeff Adams**

To justify an offer, an REO must make sense well beyond the dollars and cents. Chapter 6 described how to research your market, and Chapter 8 described where to find the best REOs in your target area. Now that you've narrowed the field of choices, it's time to closely evaluate the top contenders.

Of course, any analysis has to happen in double time because as soon as a property comes on the market, you need to move quickly with an offer, if warranted. This is the first-day-out approach, which usually works well in your favor. Adding to the urgency, it's a good rule to make as many offers as possible on as many properties as possible that fit your criteria.

That may sound like a daunting task, but it doesn't have to be if you have a power team and if you follow a few simple steps. The more deals you make, the more familiar you become with the process, and the easier the analysis becomes.

WORK WITH THE WALL MAP

Remember in Chapter 6 when I suggested you put the map of your target market on a corkboard on the wall? As you do more research and learn more about the area and various properties in it, you should be building your map database. If you discover something positive or negative about a house or neighborhood, for example, write a note and stick-pin it to the corresponding spot on the map. Eventually your map should indicate the hot market areas and cold ones; the crime areas; schools; employers; the length of time properties generally are on the market, called days on market (DOM); and lots more.

> Your wall map of your target market—your database—is the window through which you can quickly see what's happening in and around your investment area.

For evaluating potential deals, the map is invaluable. A glance can help you quickly see that an area is bad and a deal there isn't worth pursuing, or that a property is in a good location and worth another look. As you continue to evaluate and price potential deals, you'll also add more notes on home prices to the map. Eventually the map will become your guide not only to locating the best properties but also to estimating prices on comparable properties.

If you name any address in my playing field—my target market—I can tell you the approximate property value within $10,000. Get your stick-pin business going, and your map will help you make such price estimates, too.

ELEMENTS OF EVALUATING A DEAL

A property listing may seem like a great deal on paper, but reality is something else entirely. The only way to know for sure is to do your homework. You must understand your local market—the hot and the not-so-hot zones, the types of houses that sell and the types that don't, the current local market conditions, competitive pricing, and more. In other words, you and your power team must work together to evaluate deals quickly, efficiently, and without emotion.

Profit and Price

REO investors—and real estate investors in general—make their money when they buy their properties. A good purchase price for the right property in the right area guarantees a resale profit.

Do not rely on market appreciation to ensure your profits. Build your profits into any offer you make, because even though some markets have stabilized, others are still trending downward.

Be Aware of Market Conditions

When analyzing potential deals, you must be aware of the number and type of properties on the market in your target area at that moment. Markets can change swiftly, so it's important to be up-to-date. How does the current market compare with several months ago and with a year earlier? The answers to those questions—from studying the MLS listings, talking to title companies and real estate agents, and checking real estate websites—will give you an idea of very localized market trends. In almost every town or city at any given time, there are areas that simply aren't selling, and there are hot spots. Your ideal goal should be to find an REO at a great price in one of those hot spots. Perhaps mark those hot spots on your map by zip codes. That also makes it easier to quickly find properties in the hot areas.

It's important to know the current median price per square foot of homes in your target area, too. That's a quick way to see how any offer you might make on a property stacks up with the competition—other recently sold properties in the area. Your real estate agent or title company on your power team should be able to provide those numbers for you. Alternatively, you can contact local real estate and Realtor organizations as well as check online. Sites like Trulia (www.trulia.com) allow you to search pricing trends by state, city, and zip code but may not be specific enough for your needs.

Regular Inventory

Take the time to review past sales data for a target market. Typically how many properties have been on the market in the last 60, 180, and 365 days? If the number of listings and sales has been fairly stable, then you can assume the area has regular inventory. Areas with regular inventory offer great opportunities for real estate investors over the long term.

In contrast, an area with an irregular supply of homes is more difficult and riskier from an investment standpoint. For example, a recently built tract of homes or condominiums may have a rash of foreclosures in a short time. That creates an irregular spike in properties on the market for an extended period, and that drives down prices at best and at worst can leave an investor holding a property he can't sell or rent.

Properties That Sell and Those That Don't

Just as you initially culled your list of REOs in your target market, it's time to narrow the shortened list again. I advocate making offers on every suitable REO that comes on the market in your target area. That does not include properties that are hard to sell, that investors don't want, or that don't make sense.

Hard to Sell

An easy way to check if a house is hard to sell is to review the Multiple Listing Service (MLS) listing. If the average home in the area sells in 30 to 60 days, and a property has been on the market for more than 100 days, be wary. An honest listing agent may share the truth about the listing. But do your own due diligence to be sure.

Investors Don't Want Them

If the majority of investors don't want a property, there's usually a good reason. Perhaps they can't obtain financing for the property and/or the home has serious code violations. Financing can be tough to obtain for very old homes because of their physical condition, location, or similar concerns (in a flood or fire zone, for example). Serious code violations can include hazardous electrical or plumbing and illegal add-ons or alterations. Unless you have the financial resources and expertise to solve these problems, it's usually best to leave these properties alone, no matter how good the deal sounds. Major repairs on these properties quickly turn into profit-eating monsters.

Don't Make Sense

No matter how attractive a home or how good a deal, some houses simply don't make sense for an investor. That includes overbuilt homes (a newer two-story home in a neighborhood of one-story homes), most houses in commercial or industrial areas, or a luxurious home in an area of modest ones.

Palaces

In today's market with so many high- and higher-end homes that have ended up as REOs, an investor may be tempted to pick up a big property at a small price. Before doing so, however, verify how long the property has been on the market, how many times the list price has dropped, and how you might be able to sell or flip the property in the down market. No matter how good the price may sound on an REO, if you can't flip it—or show how you intend to make a profit—it's likely the property doesn't make financial sense.

Recognize Your Buyers

In evaluating potential deals, you must ask yourself if the property will appeal to your target buyer. Buyers who are investors generally like newer three- and four-bedroom homes with multiple bathrooms—homes that can command higher rents. But, as we discussed in Chapter 6, if you're planning to resell a property at retail to a first-time homebuyer, you must consider whether the home and its location are attractive to young families with children. No matter how good the deal appears on paper, if it doesn't fit the needs of your target market, then it doesn't make financial sense—unless, of course, you already have a buyer lined up and waiting with cash in hand.

Properties That Also Make Sense

If your exit strategy involves flipping a property, a deal price should have sufficient spread between the purchase price of the property and its after-repair value (ARV). If you're planning to buy and hold a property as a rental and for appreciation, you may be willing to pay more for the property as long as the monthly rental rates make sense today (positive cash flow) as well as into the future.

Similarly, buying a run-down but sound property in a nicer neighborhood usually is a smart investment strategy because the current value and potential for future appreciation are enhanced by the quality of the neighborhood. After repair, it becomes a solid investment.

Look for the ugly houses in nice areas, pick them up for a great price, and then fix them up.

Personal Inspection and Clues from the Electric Meter (or Lack Thereof)

Go see the properties that you're seriously considering as an investment. If you really know your target market, you may even already be familiar with the property. Sometimes I can pass up a property because I already know it's run-down or in a bad location. If you have a trusted real estate agent, he or she can check out the property in person, too.

Location

Is the property in a location that will be easy to flip or rent? It may be a great property and price, but if it's next to the freeway or in the middle of an industrial area, it's probably not a good investment. If a property is bordered by power lines, automatically knock $30,000 off the price. More important, though, before making an offer, be realistic about the likelihood of flipping the property or turning it into a good rental. Power lines can be toxic even to the best deal.

Workable Condition

Does the house appear to be in workable condition—that is, within your repair budget and requiring only minor and cosmetic improvements as opposed to a complete rehab? Replacing the appliances is workable. Completely gutting a bathroom and kitchen can add up to big costs if you're just starting out.

Is the Electric Meter Missing?

Check to see if the electric meter has been pulled. It's usually located on the exterior of the property in the back somewhere. When a bank repossesses a property, the city or municipality typically sends out a building inspector, who will pull the meter if there are any code violations. The violation could be as simple as trash on the property, broken windows, or a roof installed without a permit. But it also could be a substandard property addition built without a permit or something else equally serious, which can be expensive. If the electric meter is gone, call the building department to find out why.

As a new investor, I bought an old Victorian property that needed repairs, including a new roof. We hadn't pulled a permit for the new roof and were halfway through installing it when the building inspector drove by and told us to stop all work. Apparently the roof did not meet current building code standards. So we had to pull off the entire roof, make adjustments to bring it up to present building code requirements, and then reinstall the new roof. The extra work meant an additional $20,000 in repairs!

CHECKING TITLE AND OTHER POTENTIAL PROBLEMS

Don't believe everything you read about a property online, on its title, in an MLS listing, or in a seller's brochure. The information isn't always accurate, and that's not always the fault of the listing agent or service. Price aside, you need to verify as much as possible about a property, which is a big reason for personal inspections as well as double-checking documents and information conveyed throughout the REO process.

Price Complications

Look for investor-friendly real estate agents you can count on to do quality work. Too often when it comes to pricing an REO, running a comp on a property, or doing a broker price opinion (BPO), an agent will rely on the computer and never visually inspect a property. The bottom line is that before you finalize a deal, make sure you visually inspect the property.

My Foreclosure Academy instructor Zack Childress has a great example of the difference seeing a property can make when it comes to pricing a property. One of his associates was interested in a property in Decatur, Georgia. Prices of comparable properties in the area valued the home at $80,000, and the bank had listed it for sale at $69,000. Sounds fair so far, right? On the surface, perhaps, but there's more. Childress's associate had seen the property and knew the price wasn't grounded in reality. The house was literally falling down. The floors had collapsed; the bathtub had fallen through the bathroom floor, and the walls were coming down. The house was worth far less than the supposed bargain price of $69,000.

Instead of taking the time to visually inspect the property himself, or even pay someone else to do so, the agent had relied on computer-based comps to price the property. Once the bank was made aware of the real condition of the home, the investor was able to pick it up for far less than the $69,000 list price.

Verify Title with the MLS

Before you decide to make an offer on a property, always run a quick verification of the property listing on the MLS, for example, and against the property's title. Make sure they both say the same thing. They very well may not. For example, the MLS might list a property with large square footage and only one or two bedrooms, while the title says it's a three-bedroom house. That discrepancy should be a red flag to an investor. Maybe at one point a bedroom was converted into something else, the house was reconfigured, or an addition was built. Make sure that a permit, if necessary, is on file for the construction. Otherwise it could be costly for you to repair the property and/or tear out an illegal addition or add-on. You may want to consider passing on buying such a property.

On the flip side, though, an additional bedroom can substantially increase the value of a property. A three-bedroom, two-bath or even one-bath home generally can be easier to flip or rent than a two-bedroom property.

In cases where the MLS and the title differ, it's best to contact the appropriate city or county building department for details on permits on the property, or go to the local courthouse and pull tax records to help sort out and verify any discrepancies. Your title company also may be able to help you verify the data. Alternatively, property profiles may be available from websites like DataQuick (www.dataquick.com) and RealQuest (www.realquest.com).

RED FLAG WARNING

If a property's description on the MLS does not match its formal description on its title, find out why not. Make sure any remodeling and/or expansion of the property has the necessary building permits, or you could face big (and crippling) expenses.

PROPERTY INSPECTION FORM*

Property Number _____   Square Footage _____
Property Address _____   Bedrooms _____
City/State _____   Baths _____
Lot Size _____

Neighborhood:
Appearance _____   Negatives _____
Price Range _____   Positives _____

Condition of Property:
Major Repairs: _____
_____
_____
_____

Minor Repairs:
_____
_____
_____

Estimate to Repair: _____
Retail Value: _____   Max. Bid/Offer: _____

*For a downloadable, customizable version, log on to www.jeffadamsforms.com.

Partnering for Success

If you work with a partner—your spouse, for example—be clear on the responsibilities of each partner when it comes to analyzing potential deals. Otherwise, no matter how well the two of you get along, important things can fall through the cracks.

PRICING A PROPERTY AS BUYER OR SELLER

The accurate valuation of an investment property—whether as a buyer or seller—is crucial. It helps determine offer prices and sale prices, profit margins, rehab considerations, rents, and more. To buy an REO and flip it or rent it for a solid profit, you as an investor must be able to price the property accurately when you buy it from the bank and when you sell it or rent it out.

Let's examine various aspects of valuing a property.

ARV Is Crucial

Central to valuing a property is its after-repair value (ARV). The ARV should be an accurate assessment—as opposed to an inflated number based on wishful thinking. The calculations must be grounded in realistic market and economic assessments, which is one more reason the predeal research is so very important for an REO investor.

As part of determining the ARV, ask the question "What are similar properties selling for?" You must know the answer in order to accurately determine your potential property's ARV. If an exit strategy calls for flipping a property at retail, that ARV likely will become the selling price, too.

Understanding REO Repairs

Learn to quickly ascertain what, if anything, needs to be done to a property you're considering buying. You or your rehabber should be able to determine that in a 10-minute walkthrough. Be sensible and conservative in your repair estimates. How much work does the property really need?

You're not going for a state-of-the-art *Architectural Digest* makeover. Repairing REO properties to flip and/or to rent calls for doing the minimum required to bring a property up to competitive standards when compared with similar properties in the area. Forget the granite countertops; composite works fine. Likewise, opt for a standard door, not the fancy one. By keeping the cost of repairs to a minimum, you can flip the property quickly and for a profit.

A quick and accurate way to estimate repair costs is to bring in the handyman or rehabber on your power team. Usually in a few minutes a handyman can ballpark the cost of the work. When I have to make a quick judgment myself on whether to make an offer on a property, I usually rank the repairs:

- Lots of work.
- Medium work.
- Little or no work.

Lots of work is a complete gut of the interior of a property or a complete new kitchen. Medium work might be a new roof or new windows. Little or no work calls for perhaps a quick interior paint job or new carpet, if that.

In Chapter 7 I suggested a field trip to your local home improvement superstore to learn about and record the costs of various home repairs and improvements. Here's where the notes you took come into play.

As mentioned earlier, a good rule of thumb for beginning investors is to steer clear of the major rehabs until you have a bit more experience with the unexpected costs and complications of REO investing.

Where Is Your Profit?

To accurately calculate your profit requires an assessment of the numbers associated with a property acquisition, its repair, costs associated with holding the property, and the expense of selling or renting it. Let's take a closer look:

- Acquisition costs (total costs associated with purchasing a property; can include title fees, escrow or closing attorney and lender fees, and various other charges).
- Dollar amount of repairs and upgrades needed to make property competitive on market.
- Holding costs (including interim monthly payments, taxes, insurance, utilities, and miscellaneous expenses).
- Sales costs (real estate commissions, escrow or closing attorney, and title fees, and any other costs associated with selling the property).

Add up all these costs, then subtract them from the ARV, and you end up with your estimated profit. If it's not enough to justify your efforts, then lower your offer price. I like to make a minimum 10 percent profit on any deal.

Don't be greedy. Be sensible, and look at a deal with prices in mind that move properties quickly. If you pick up an REO for $50,000 and its ARV is $100,000, consider flipping it wholesale to another investor for $65,000; you'll turn it quickly and still make some money on the deal after expenses. It's far better to make less profit on many deals than no profit on zero deals.

Comps

To determine the value of a property and its sales price, you'll need to consider prices of comparable properties (comps) in the area. You'll need to draw on your research of the target area, as well as create your own comparative market analysis (CMA) that compares a property to similar properties in the area.

With potential REO deals, you don't have time for and don't want the expense of detailed CMAs. But you still can quickly and easily determine the price. As mentioned earlier, some MLS listings have a feature that shows property locations and costs by location. If you're not sure that you're comparing like properties,

don't overlook talking to real estate agents in the area for their assessments and advice. All comps, though, aren't created equal. When figuring a comp:

- Use at least two different sources—the MLS and your title company, for example. (Work at developing relationships so that you have access to title company comps; that data is invaluable.) No matter how many properties you include, the MLS is not enough by itself. It has data only on those properties listed and sold by MLS members. Private-party sales, intrafamily transactions, third-party foreclosure sales, and the like are not included in MLS data, yet all affect property values. Comps from a title company, however, encompass all properties. Use third-party websites. A few include RealQuest (www.realquest.com), Zillow (www.zillow.com), Trulia (www.trulia.com), Redfin (www.redfin.com), and Cyberhomes (www.cyberhomes.com). Also look at local and regional sites. If using two or more sites, make sure the original sources of the data are different. Also be careful that the comps are accurate. Numbers from sites like Zillow and Cyberhomes can sometimes be way off because they're too general and not specific to a particular market.
- Include only homes that have sold in the last 90 days. Markets change too quickly to use older sales. Prices may have gone up— or down—so make sure the comps are current.
- Drive by other comparable properties on the market to get a feel for how a particular property stacks up against its competition.

Don't forget to add pricing data on various properties to your wall map. Remember, you're building your database one stick-pinned note at a time.

Understanding the Math

Not everyone is a math wizard who quickly can figure the differences or percent changes between prices and offers, or ARVs and list prices, or even offer and list prices. Luckily, the Internet, personal computers, cell phones, and handheld calculators make everyone's life with numbers a bit easier. As an investor, you do need to know how to work with the numbers, so figure out what you don't know and get the help you need.

If percentages confound you, go to the Internet and try Math.com (www.math.com), specifically its three-way percentage calculator (www.math.com/students/calculators/source/3percent.htm), or eHow (www.ehow.com). Alternatively, head to the nearest gadget store and pick up a calculator that can figure percentages. Many cell phones have built-in calculators or a downloadable app that can help, too.

HOW TO FIGURE A PROPERTY'S COST PER SQUARE FOOT

Market value of home/Square footage of home = Cost per square foot

Example:

Market value of home: $125,000

Square footage of home: 2,500

Cost per square foot = $125,000/2,500 = $50

Cost per Square Foot

Your analysis of similar properties also should include the cost per square foot of each of those comparables and of any property you're considering buying. To determine that, divide the market value by the square footage:

Market value of home/Square footage of home = Cost per square foot

To determine the average cost per square foot of comparable properties, add their prices per square foot, then divide by the total number of properties. For example, if you use two comparables (House A and House B):

House A's price per square foot + House B's price per square foot = Total price per square foot

Total price per square foot/2 = Average price per square foot

Another useful number to understand and calculate is the price per square foot of an REO. That's done by determining the average cost per square foot of the comparable properties (see earlier) and then multiplying that by the square footage of the REO:

For example, if an REO property is 3,500 square feet and the average price per square foot of comparables is $60, then the ARV of the REO is $210,000:

$$3,500 \times \$60 = \$210,000$$

More on understanding the math in REO buying and selling is given in the Addendum at back of the book.

Chapter 12

HOW TO MAKE AN OFFER AND NEGOTIATE WITH BANKS

Your first offer on a property is like a first date, not a marriage proposal.
     —**Zack Childress, successful real estate investor and Jeff Adams, Foreclosure Academy instructor**

Though it does not seal the deal, a first offer on a property can open the door. Savvy REO investors make sure the first offer is done right so that it will get them in the game. You can't win if you're not playing the game! Getting into the game should be your immediate goal. Believe it or not, 80 to 90 percent of all offers submitted on REOs in today's market end up in the trash because the people submitting those offers don't know what they're doing. People don't know how to fill out and submit complete offers.

When I first started out investing in REOs, I was sitting in the office of an REO agent when an offer came in on the fax. She glanced at it and then quickly tossed it into the trash.

I asked her, "Why did you do that?"

Her response: "I don't have time for these looky loos."

I looked at the offer, which was from a well-known real estate guru. The contract included a contingency clause stating that the offer was subject to interior inspection. If you as an REO investor want to get your offers accepted, they must be clean, without contingencies, and with all the necessary documentation, including a proof of funds letter.

RULES OF THE GAME

In the highly competitive arena of REO investing, it's important to gear your approach and your offers toward the widely accepted norms. Don't rock the boat. Learn to play the game by its established rules, and you'll come out a winner. Otherwise your offers end up in the trash!

What to Avoid

One of the quickest ways to guarantee that your offers will end up in the wastebasket is to make generic offers on properties without any research on the particular property. A perfect example is a lowball offer on a property that, had the investor taken the time to look, he or she already would have known was heavily discounted. Most would-be investors make generic offers or blind offers because that's what many REO investing programs teach. Those types of offers, however, are pet peeves for many already overworked REO agents.

Another kiss of death to your investing success is failing to close on your offers after they're accepted. Getting cold feet about a deal isn't acceptable unless your gut and every other guidepost—including the statistics and comps—tell you a deal is all wrong. Banks want to deal with investors who follow through on their promises and close on deals. If you submit an offer and it's accepted, you had better close on the deal or have a very good reason to back out (more on that later), or you'll end up with a bad reputation and your offers will be tossed out.

RED FLAG WARNING

Forget the contingencies or your offers will end up in the trash!

If you show a bank and its REO agent that you're a serious investor who is fair, who knows what to do and how to do it, and who can quickly close on deals, the deals will come your way. That approach achieves your goal of persuading agents to turn to you first with the best deals.

Forget the Contingencies

Banks don't like contracts with contingencies. If REO offers are saddled with contingencies, they'll end up in the trash. A few of those devil-in-the-details contingencies that doom most contracts without so much as a cursory look by REO agents, let alone get them submitted to banks, include:

- Subject to interior inspection.
- Subject to a partner's approval.
- Subject to property repairs.
- Subject to loan approval.
- Subject to termite inspection.

In other words, your offers should be up front and without strings attached; your offer should include the phrase "as is" or "where is." Ever since I figured that out and changed the way I handle my offers, I've had tremendous success in getting offers accepted.

Make Lots of Offers

Real estate investing is a numbers game, and in this game it takes many offers to buy a few properties. If you're not making offers, and lots of them, you're not making any money.

As an investor, the goal is to acquire properties at a wholesale price. Consequently, your offers typically will be low compared with the after-repair value (ARV) of the home. That means you can expect to get a lot of turndowns on your offers. However, when a motivated buyer (you) meets a motivated seller (the bank), the result can be a very profitable deal.

ELEMENTS OF YOUR OFFER

Every REO offer you make to an agent or bank—or that your agent makes on your behalf—should include the following:

- **Cover letter.** One page; describes who you are and summarizes your offer.
- **Cash offer with earnest money.** Gives details of your offer plus a photocopy of an earnest-money check (typically payable to escrow or the closing attorney, though it varies).
- **Proof of funds letter.** Should be within the last 30 days.
- **No contingencies or weasel clauses.**

Submit All the Necessary Documentation

If a good REO comes on the market, the listing agent is likely to receive many offers within the first few days of the listing. To ensure that your offer has a good chance of getting accepted, make it complete and provide all the necessary documentation. Incomplete offers quickly end up in the trash.

I recently closed on a great REO deal in Rialto, California. The property's ARV was $240,000, and I up picked the house for $159,900. After I submitted my offer the listing agent called to tell me the house was mine if I could close in the next 15 days. Apparently they received four offers on the house, but mine was the only "clean" one—forms filled out completely with all the necessary paperwork attached.

We talk more about the details of the right documentation in Chapter 13.

Standard State Contract

It's up to the real estate agent on your power team to write your offers and submit them to the REO agents for consideration. However, I've made some of my best deals when the REO listing agent actually writes the offer for me on their property—I go directly to the agent instead of through someone else. In those cases, the agent has extra incentive to close the deal because he or she then receives commission as both listing and selling agent. Many REO agents, though, especially the volume sellers, often are so swamped with properties that they can't or won't write offers for you.

Meanwhile, I also work to build relationships with REO agents with the goal of them sending me a "pre-list" of their REO deals. These are REOs that have not yet come on the market. I have several REO agents that send me weekly e-mails of these pre-list REOs.

My agent can make offers quickly on many properties at once because I use a preprinted offer form that starts with the standard real estate contract for the state where I'm investing. Your real estate agent should have a copy of such contracts; sometimes they're also available online from your state Department of Real Estate. Just make sure that the contract is specific to your market area's state.

Fill in the contract with the necessary data, including your signature (and initial each page), but leave the property address and dollar amount of the offer blank. When a solid REO comes on the market and you want to make an offer, all you need to do is call your agent, who in turn takes the preprinted form, plugs in the property address and the amount of the cash offer, packages the form with a preprinted and signed cover letter and proof-of-funds letter, and then submits it to the REO agent. It's fast, clean, and thorough. Best of all, it takes only a few minutes.

Don't forget to make sure that your agent follows up with the REO agent listing the property to make sure the offer was received.

A Note about Earnest Money

Earnest money shows the seller that you're a serious investor. It's a commitment demonstrating that by submitting an offer, you have the funds to follow through and close the deal if your offer is accepted.

I recommend $5,000 as earnest money. If you can afford only $1,000, that's okay, too. Typically, earnest money should be at least 1 percent of the offer price.

You do *not* send the actual check. Instead, send a photocopy of the check made payable to the third party that will handle the closing. It varies by state, and can be an escrow or title company—or closing attorney, depending on your state's laws. A copy of the one check can be used to make multiple offers. If an offer is accepted, the actual check is then sent usually within three to seven days after acceptance of the offer.

Exit Strategies and Contracts

Your exit strategy for a property can affect the way a contract or offer is worded because laws and rules related to property acquisition, tax ramifications, and so on vary by state. I'm not a legal expert or tax adviser, so check with both to determine the best approach when writing your offers.

If, on the one hand, I plan to flip or rent a property, I usually make the offer on a property in the name of my corporation or a land trust.

That provides me with a layer of asset protection. If, on the other hand, I'm wholesaling a property, I may do a simultaneous closing depending on the laws of the state where the property is located. In Florida, for example, simultaneous closings are common, while in California they're rare.

The key, though, is to get your first deal done. It may make more sense to do a deal in your own name, and then worry about the asset protection aspects later. That's what I did when I first started out.

Building Relationships with REO Agents

To be successful, you must learn to build relationships with REO agents. An ongoing relationship often means getting insider information about a property and its pricing, along with first access to the best deals in your market.

I've worked with one REO agent for 10 years. We have developed an excellent working relationship, and she typically brings me great deals even before they're listed on the MLS. For example, she approached me about a property in my target market, which includes Rialto, California. I drove out to see it and ran some of the numbers. The property needed some repairs, but other houses in the neighborhood were selling in the low $200,000s. I came back with an offer for $130,000. The bank countered with $133,000, and we sealed the deal that afternoon—and before the property ever hit the MLS.

Developing a relationship with an REO agent starts with making sure your offers are professional and contain all the necessary information. Be honest and straightforward with agents and their employers—banks. Banks don't like surprises. If you're up front, they'll come back to you.

Before your agent sends an offer, make sure he or she calls or e-mails the agent to say that the offer is coming.

Always Follow Up Again

After your agent has submitted an offer, make sure he or she follows up 24 to 48 hours later by contacting the listing agent to confirm receipt of the offer.

He or she also should ask what the best offer received to date is to determine if you're in the ballpark or not. If your bid is in the acceptable range, he or she should ask how your offer could be enhanced in order for it to be accepted (increase your deposit, for example). Your agent should continue to follow up—usually at least once a week—to find out the status of your offer. Even if your offer isn't accepted, your agent should ask if the REO agent has any other properties that might interest you.

THE INSPECTION CONUNDRUM OR NOT

Weasel (contingency) clauses are not acceptable in your offers, period. Make sure your offer specifically states that there is no inspection contingency. For many beginning REO investors, that's a big stumbling block, especially the idea of writing an offer on a property without making it contingent on a home inspection. After all, if we're buying our own home, inspections are a crucial final contingency.

Don't sweat this lack of an inspection clause in your initial offer. Most times, a bank's counteroffer or a contract stemming from your offer will contain an addendum that includes time for an inspection. Also, the time it takes to arrange the closing—usually about five to seven days—is enough for a home inspection.

If you find something wrong with the property during that time, and it's a deal breaker—perhaps lots of black mold or unpermitted room additions that you weren't aware of and don't want to deal with— you do have recourse. Even if you suddenly get very cold feet and there's no way you will go through with the deal, there are a number of legitimate ways to back out of a deal gracefully.

LEGITIMATE EXCUSES TO GET OUT OF A CONTRACT

Up until now in this book, the goal has been to get your offer on an REO accepted. But there are legitimate reasons why you might want to back out of a contract, and efficient ways to do so.

Condition of the Property

Always inspect the property after your offer has been accepted and before the deal closes. If the condition of the property has deteriorated since your offer was accepted by the bank, you can notify the bank of that. For example, the property could have been vandalized, the roof could have begun to leak, termites could have infested the property, or the septic system could have backed up. (Also as mentioned earlier, these could be reasons to request a reduced price for the property.)

Closing Delayed

Banks often fail to close on time. That's especially true today with so many REOs on the market, along with title and foreclosure complications. Nonetheless, if the bank doesn't close on time, pulling out of the deal is perfectly legitimate. Simply send an e-mail to the escrow company, title company, or closing attorney—whichever is handling the transaction—on the afternoon that the property is scheduled to close, stating that you would like your deposit back because the bank did not close in the required time frame. Follow up with a phone call to make sure they received the e-mail.

Be careful with this tactic, though. If you use it too often, you will get a bad reputation for pulling out of deals.

Seller Disclosures

Investors who want the option to pull out of a deal may write in the contract, "Seller disclosures to be delivered within five days of acceptance of offer." As with delayed closings, it's almost impossible for banks, overwhelmed by REOs, to comply with this demand. Technically if the bank doesn't comply, it would be in violation of the contract and the deal could therefore be voided.

However, this is one more weasel clause, so I advise people not to make this demand. If you inspect a property before you make an offer, you'll know about problems with the property and what to offer.

I made an offer on a property and the bank accepted it. But, during the escrow process, I discovered that the house had a faulty septic system and would need to be connected to the city's sewer system. That would mean an additional $15,000 out of my pocket, so I went back to the bank and negotiated a drastically reduced price for the property. If I had decided the sewer hook-up cost was too much to make the deal worthwhile, I also could have pulled out of the contract due to the lack of seller disclosure.

CODE VIOLATIONS

An investor's discovery of code violations that the bank refuses to correct also could be just cause for pulling out of a deal. On top of that, with so many homes in foreclosure and as REOs, many local governments have passed laws creating stiff fines and penalties for financial institutions that fail to maintain their REO properties. The city of Los Angeles, California, for example, can fine the financial institution if its properties are not maintained. You should contact the local building department prior to closing to find out if any major code violations or fines have been levied against a property.

LEGITIMATE EXCUSES TO DELAY A CLOSING

Occasionally an investor needs an extension before closing on a property. There may be financial difficulties, or there may be something seriously wrong with a property that requires more time to evaluate. With so many REOs today, delays are commonplace.

Whatever the investor's reason for needing an extension, the bank requires a valid excuse. A request for more time won't be granted without extenuating circumstances.

Financing Issues

Lender Delays

Problems stemming from lender delays are frequent with the rush of REO sales in today's market. Don't count on this delay, though, or you could get caught unexpectedly. If your deal gets caught behind scores of others and faces delays, be sure to get a statement in writing from the lender.

Title Delays

It's the same with title companies. Some companies are swamped with work and sometimes can't keep up. Again, get the reason for the closing delay in writing from the title company and present it to the REO agent along with your request for an extension on the closing date.

Appraisal Issues

An appraisal may raise additional issues—verification of square footage, possible missing building permits or zoning concerns, for example—that require additional time to clarify. If that happens, ask for the additional time.

Insurance Issues

Delays in closing also can be the result of the inability to insure a property in, say, a rural area or in a location susceptible to fires or floods. Again, if that's the case, this is a legitimate reason, so ask for an extension.

Code Violations

As mentioned earlier, before closing, check with the city or county to make sure a vacant home you're purchasing does not have any major code violations. These kinds of violations can be very costly and eat into your profit margins.

Lender-Required Repairs

Occasionally a lender, even a hard-money one, may require certain repairs to a property before providing cash for closing. It could be the result of health and safety issues or something else.

KEYS TO SUCCESSFUL NEGOTIATION

Don't be afraid to negotiate. The more you practice negotiating, the less daunting it will become. Incorporate a few negotiating tips and tricks, and soon the process will become second nature. Keep in mind, too, that REO agents don't get paid to answer questions. They get paid to close deals. That means you should consider the following:

- **Know the details.** Do your homework about a property ahead of time so that the agent knows you're a serious investor who can close a deal quickly and cleanly.
- **Have supporting data to justify your offer.** Don't simply make a lowball offer without pointing out your reasons why.
- **Stick to your price parameters.** Don't lose sight of your predetermined maximum price for a property. Be realistic in determining that dollar amount, too.

Steps to Negotiation

Negotiating becomes simpler if you understand the parts to the process. Basically there are three steps: relationship, prenegotiation, and the negotiation itself.

The first step is the relationship, which begins when you initially interact with an REO agent and try to build a rapport or at least common ground. You could begin with a phone call to the agent who might expect a lowball offer from you. Instead, introduce yourself as an investor who is willing to pay a fair price for REO properties in your market, and is interested in receiving a list of the agent's pre-list REOs on a regular basis.

The second step is prenegotiation, when you talk with the agent about your interest in making an offer on a property they have listed, whether there are any other offers on the property, and the lowest price the bank would be willing to accept.

The third step occurs after you've made an offer and are negotiating the terms.

Tips and Tricks

Following are some basic negotiating tactics that can help in any negotiations, including with REO agents:

- Listen carefully to what's being said, and to your gut feelings.

- Promises are the foundation for your reputation. If you agree to something, make sure it gets done and in the time frame promised, if not sooner.
- Always ask open-ended questions during negotiations, and avoid declarative sentences.
- Never burn your bridges. Always be polite but firm. Don't become angry or lose control while negotiating.
- Don't be afraid of silence.
- He who mentions price first loses.
- When someone answers no, ask "Why not?"
- Frame your questions to obtain the answers you want. People are much more motivated to respond with a "no" than a "yes." Make that "no" mean "yes" by the way you pose your question. For example, "Is there any reason why you wouldn't consider . . . ?"
- Be aware of body language; it reveals subconscious thoughts and feelings. (Don't cross your arms in front of your chest; it conveys combativeness.)

LEGITIMATE REASONS FOR PRICE REDUCTIONS

In today's market, list prices on REOs are not always firm. Chapter 11 described how an agent might incorrectly price a property because he or she didn't do a visual inspection. Some other legitimate reasons to lower your offer on a property (as long as you have supporting data) are the following:

- **Title issues.** For example, you may be able to get a $1,000 to $5,000 price reduction by allowing the transaction to close with a lien such as a code violation on the title. You will have to check with the city first to verify the violation is a minor one.
- **Condition of property.** If the property has been vandalized or has deteriorated in some way since you signed the contract, you have a case to ask for a further price reduction.

Respond to Counteroffers

Time is of the essence in an REO negotiation. Respond immediately to any counteroffer or a request for your highest and best offer from the bank. In the case of the latter, a bank might get a number of similar offers on a property and come back to those people asking for their best offer. Many of the offers likely were blind; the people making them won't want to bother with the extra effort of making another offer, and therefore they drop out. That means less competition for the property.

Never ignore a highest and best offer request. Don't, however, lose sight of the comparable properties (comps), the reasoning behind your original offer, and your profit needs. Approach your response with the following in mind:

- **Reevaluate your numbers.** Your initial offer encompassed factors like property values, repair estimate, financing costs, and estimated holding costs. Make sure the deal still makes sense to you.
- **Verify your comparables.** The real estate market is in constant flux. Comps from 60 to 90 days ago may have changed significantly, so revisit your comparable prices to make sure they're in tune with the current market.
- **Respond quickly.** Your competition is responding quickly, so make sure you do, too.
- **Fill out all the requested paperwork.** Do so completely and quickly (more on the right paperwork in Chapter 13) to make sure you don't lose a property to your competition.
- **Attach a new page if adjusting an offer.** If you decide to adjust your offer, be sure to attach a new "Page 1 of Offer." If you don't resubmit your first page with the updated number, the offer may be overlooked or even tossed in the trash.

Even if you choose not to make another offer or can't go any higher in price and actually have to go lower, get back to the REO agent immediately. Thank him or her for the opportunity, and indicate this is the best price you can do.

GETTING THE PAPERWORK RIGHT

Chapter 13

GETTING THE
PAPERWORK RIGHT

You have only a few initial seconds to grab an REO agent's attention. Make them count.

—Jeff Adams

To get ahead and stay ahead of the competition, you must get the paperwork right. Surprisingly, bad paperwork squelches more deals than you might imagine. To make sure your offers aren't undermined by paperwork that comes up short, pay attention to the details throughout the REO buying process. That means you must get the funding right; do your research thoroughly; choose the right properties; analyze the numbers correctly using the most up-to-date and accurate comps; make spot-on offers with the necessary documentation, and follow through and close deals. That's how to bury the competition.

Let's look more closely at some of the best strategies related to completing the necessary paperwork and documentation throughout the REO purchase and sales process.

SMOOTH FUNDING

After a lender agrees to work with you—and long before you start your search for the right REOs—the company should send you specific instructions on the process involved in funding your deals, including providing you with a proof of funds letter. If your cash is to come from a private individual, family members, or friends, it's important to have formal documentation of the process involved, including the length of time between "request for funding" for a particular deal and "delivery of cash." Both you and the lender—whoever it is—must be clear on the steps and the processes involved.

You'll also need a formal funding request form to fill out when and if a bank accepts an offer on a specific REO.

Together these documents will help ensure the smooth and timely transfer of cash to close your deals swiftly.

SAMPLE FUNDING AGREEMENT INSTRUCTIONS*

GetYourCash.com
123 Main Street, Anywhere, USA 12345
Phone: 123-123-1234
Fax: 321-321-4321

E-mail: info@GetYourCash.com

Funding and Agreement Instructions

Congratulations on working with GetYourCash.com. We look forward to funding your upcoming deals and working with you to make sure that everything goes as expected. First, please take a moment to read all the items below. Doing so will give you a better understanding of what is expected so that we can fund your deal.

- All fields of the Funding Request MUST be completed, legibly and accurately. Missing information will result in delaying your funding request.
- All required supporting documentation MUST be submitted together with the Funding Request and Fund Agreement.
- Please do NOT submit any documentation until your purchase and sale is scheduled.
- Funding will typically be available 5 (five) to 7 (seven) business days from the date of receipt and acceptance of all required documentation.
- If more than 1 (one) Attorney and/or Closing Agent is participating in the closing, please print a separate Funding Agreement for each additional party to complete.
- Closing in the name of a business entity (Limited Liability Corporation [LLC] or Corporation, etc.) is strongly encouraged.
- E-mail submitted to info@GetYourCash.com is the preferred method of returning all documentation.

- Once the Funding Request and Funding Agreement are returned and accepted (along with all the supporting documents), a member of our team will contact you.
- Please contact our office at 123-123-1234 x12 with any questions you may have PRIOR to submitting any documentation.

Best Regards,
M. Cash

Sample Funding Request*

Name: _____

Address: _____

_____

E-mail: _____

Phone: _____

Social Security No. (For Verification Only): _____

Property Address: _____

_____

Purchase Price: _____

Amount Requested: _____

Resale Price: _____

<u>Attorney and/or Closing Agent (Representing Applicant)</u>

Name: _____

Address: _____

_____

Phone/Fax/E-mail: _____

Comments: _____

Return all documentation to:

GetYourCash.com

123 Main Street, Anywhere, USA 12345

Phone: 123-123-1234

Fax: 321-321-4321

E-mail: info@GetYourCash.com

(Continued)

(Continued)

> I understand that false or misleading information given in this application will result in cancellation. I authorize investigation of all statements contained in this application that may be necessary in the funding process.
>
> _____
> Signature of Applicant   Date
> *For a downloadable, customizable version of this document, go to www.jeffadamsforms.com.

COVER LETTERS

Throughout all steps of the REO buying process—from finding the professionals to procuring funding, making offers, sealing deals, and flipping properties—initially you as an investor have only a few seconds to grab someone's attention. Make those seconds count, in person with your appearance and approach, and in writing with the help of a dynamite cover sheet or cover letter.

In Chapter 5, you saw an example of a direct and to-the-point cover letter to a potential lender. The same approach works when it comes to making an offer on a property. Pair that succinct cover letter with a clean offer and the right documentation for a winning approach.

"Quick," "clean," and "easy" are the words to keep in mind when putting together a cover letter. Keep the letter to one page so that whoever reads it will see at a glance the key information pertinent to the purpose of the letter.

A cover page for an offer on a property, for instance, should include the following:

- Buyer's name and buyer's company name, if applicable.
- Buyer's contact information, including address, phone number, and e-mail address.
- Agent's name and company name, if applicable.
- Agent's contact information, including address, phone number, and e-mail address.
- Property address, including assessor's parcel number (APN).

- Summary of offer, including amount of earnest money deposit and total offer amount, along with reasons in support of dollar amount (if, for example, an offer is well below list price due to major repairs required to bring the property up to code).
- How you will pay for the property—all cash, for example.
- State that offer is for the property "as is" and "where is," which suggests to the REO agent that your offer is not based on contingencies such as property inspection.

PROOF OF FUNDS

Proof of funds, as you've read, simply assures a bank or seller that you have the funds or access to the funds necessary to complete a deal. Submitting an offer without a proof-of-funds letter is a deal killer.

Proof of funds does not mean that you send with your offer a photocopy of a cashier's check payable to the bank for the total amount of your offer. Instead, it usually consists of a formal letter on your company letterhead that describes how the deal will be funded, along with a copy of a bank statement, individual retirement account (IRA), or anything showing you have liquid (easily accessible) assets to make the deal. If you're getting the money from a conventional lender or hard-money lender, make sure to include a copy of the proof of funds letter from that lender, which will contain information on the extent of your line of credit with the lender.

WRITING AN OFFER ON AN REO

As you've read, you will need to pick up a copy of your state's standard real estate contract as the basis for writing your offer on an REO. Every state's contract is slightly different, but many of the basics are the same.

The contracts usually are long, but take the time to fill them out completely, and sign and/or initial where necessary. Remember, you have to do this only once because you will leave blank the property address, dollar amount of the offer, closing date, and the current date, and then will photocopy the document. When a deal comes up, you— or your real estate agent—simply have to fill in the missing property address and dollar offer, date it, and send it to the appropriate REO agent, along with the necessary documentation.

Pay Attention to the Details

Some details to keep in mind about documents and how to fill them out:

- When writing cash offers, allow for a two-week closing and be sure to include the closing date on the contract.
- Once your offer has been accepted, during the two-week period when the deal is being finalized, check the property several times, because vandalism of vacant properties is rampant these days. If the property is seriously damaged after your bid was accepted and before closing, you have legitimate cause to ask for a reduced price or pull out of the deal. After closing, it's too late.
- Sometimes banks will request supplemental documents. Follow the REO agent's instructions and get them to the bank sooner rather than later. I always try to beat any deadline. Don't be discouraged by the extra paperwork. It cuts down on your competition because many investors won't bother with the extra work.
- Always fill in the contract so that it reads "all cash" (that means no closing costs), no warranty, no inspection, "as is" and "where is."
- Check the appropriate box for "No disclosures" by the seller required.
- Submit all the required paperwork the first time!
- Some standard state contracts will ask if you are the occupying party for the property. Leave the question unanswered (blank) on the form unless the bank specifically asks the question. If the bank or its agent does ask, answer honestly.
- Usually on the first page of a contract, there's a place to indicate how many days are allowed for inspection of the property after the contract is accepted. Always put in ZERO (0). An experienced REO agent will look at how you fill this out. If he sees a zero, he'll know that your offer is a clean one, that you mean business, and that you know what you're doing.

- Don't forget to sign and have your agent sign the document as well as initial all the pages. Again, don't date the document before photocopying it.
- If a property is occupied legally—for example, the bank may have rented it out in the interim before selling it—the contract should state that the property will be vacated three to five days prior to closing. Inspect the property after it's vacated and before closing to make sure no one—including squatters—is living there and that the property is in the same condition as when you agreed to purchase it. If not, go back to the negotiating table, get a reduction in price, and get the inhabitants out. Or you may want to rethink the deal entirely.

How to Take Title to a Property

To determine the best way to take title to a property—in your own name or as a corporation, limited liability company, land trust, and so on—it's best to check with your legal advisers, including your accountant, tax adviser, and attorney.

If the offer on a property is made in the name of a legal entity other than you as an individual, be sure to include in your offer packet a copy of the articles of incorporation, trust papers, or other legal document that gives you the right to sign on behalf of the entity.

Some related ideas to consider about taking title include:

- **Acquire the property in your own name.** You may want to do this if you are a beginning investor.
- **Buy and then sell a property at retail.** If you're buying a property to flip at retail, you'll eventually want to purchase your properties either in a land trust or in a corporation for the dual benefit of asset protection and tax planning.
- **Buy and then sell wholesale.** If the exit strategy on a property calls for flipping the property wholesale, you may want to buy it in the name of a land trust with you as the trustee, and then at closing assign your rights as trustee to the wholesale buyer. You

also can buy a property with a back-to-back closing where you close in your name and the end buyer closes in his or her name. This can be done without using any of your own cash or credit by using a transactional funder like Fund-A-Flip (www.fundaflip.com). They do these kinds of transactions all the time.

- **In California, use a land trust.** If a deal takes place in California, it's best to use a land trust and simply resign as the "trustee" at closing and assign the beneficial interest in the trust to your wholesale buyer. It's not difficult, and your escrow company or title company can walk you through the process.
- **Use a grant deed or a warranty deed.** If you opt to close in your name, collect your wholesale fee at closing and then use a grant deed or a warranty deed to transfer the property to your wholesale buyer. If you close in a corporation's name, use either a grant deed or a warranty deed to transfer the property to your wholesale buyer at closing and collect your "wholesale" fee.
- **Hold as a rental property for monthly cash flow.** If the plan is to buy a property, then hold and rent it, you may want to buy the property in the name of a land trust, limited liability company, or corporation for asset protection and to possibly reduce your tax liability.

Some lenders won't make loans to trusts. If that's the case, one option is to buy a property in your own name and use a grant deed or a warranty deed at closing to place it into your trust.

The suggestions here are only ideas and possibilities. Be sure to check with the appropriate experts on your power team before deciding the best approach for your situation.

CLOSING PROCESS

Once a bank has accepted your offer, the closing process begins. A lot of documentation may be involved, but consider all of it a learning (and growing your business) experience.

Bank Addendums and Disclosures

After the bank accepts your contract on a property, all the addendums and disclosures as required in the contract become additional parts of the contract. That means you are contractually obliged to comply with any new requirements in the addendums. In the state of California, for example, the Natural Hazards Disclosure Report is standard (the seller generally pays for it, about $100), and it becomes part of the contract.

Often a bank addendum will replace the state contract to the extent that some of the original terms of the contract—whether price, down payment, or closing date—have changed. All other terms that are unchanged remain as originally agreed to by both parties.

Double-check to make sure all parts of the agreement are included in the addendum. As with any contract, don't assume any negotiated items have been resolved in your favor unless you see them in writing.

Escrow/Closing Instructions

Whether the independent third party in charge of making sure all parties comply with the contractual agreement (including addendums), governing a transaction is an escrow company, title company, or closing attorney, make sure the closing date is accurate. Some REO sellers, like Fannie Mae, include a $100-per-day late penalty if the buyer doesn't close on time.

Generally the closing costs are split by buyer and seller in an REO transaction.

Preliminary Title Report

The preliminary title report addresses the condition of title as of the day the report is provided to you. You and your agent should carefully review the report early in the closing process. Although it's the independent third party's responsibility to ensure that any items of record are paid, it's best to double-check those items yourself. Items of record could include back taxes, code violations, and delinquent homeowner association dues.

Mistakes can and do happen, so verify that any potential clouds on a property's title are cleared up before the actual closing date. If they're not, you as the new owner could be liable for hefty costs. Delinquent homeowners association (HOA) dues, for example, may cost you hundreds of dollars in fines in order to bring them current.

Also, although the bank usually pays for the title insurance, ask about getting a "binder" policy (if it's available in your state) at your expense. That can save you the cost of buying another standard title policy as long as you flip the property within a certain time frame.

Other Closing Documents

Vesting Sheet

A vesting sheet is especially important if you're planning to add a buyer or if you're using a land trust, corporation, or limited liability company to buy the property. This vesting information is essential so that the documentation can be drawn up correctly ahead of time.

Grant Deed/Warranty Deed

Both grant deeds and warranty deeds guarantee that a property's title is free and clear. In the closing process, it's essential that the purchasing entity—you personally, a trust, a corporation, or another entity—be identified correctly early in the process so all the documents can be prepared properly and on time.

In the case of large corporate sellers, it can take weeks to sign and return a deed.

Other Disclosure Forms

Other disclosure forms you may need to deal with include lead paint disclosure and natural hazard disclosure (flood, fire, or earthquake zones, for example). The seller is responsible for providing these disclosures to you, and you in turn must provide them to your buyers if you flip the property.

Release of Contingencies

Make sure to verify that all prior contingencies as indicated in the title report and the contract, are satisfied and met prior to finalizing the deal. That means no contingencies should remain.

Clear Title

It may be someone else's responsibility to clear any exceptions to a property's title before closing, but it's important that you make sure it happens. Any unresolved title issues will interfere with your ability to sell the property once you take title.

SEAL THE DEAL AND BEYOND

Here are a few more caveats and concerns to keep in mind to make sure your deal goes down cleanly and smoothly, and you walk away a winner time and time again.

- If you're planning to wholesale the property, have your buyer lined up and ready to go. Any delays after you close on the purchase will cost you money.
- Make sure your financing is poised and ready to go. Despite weaker demand for loans today, don't assume your loan will be completed on time. Be proactive with your lender.
- Wire the funds at least 48 hours before the closing date. Pay attention to time differences if you're wiring money from one time zone to another; remember to consider holidays and weekends, too.
- Do one last home inspection prior to wiring those funds.
- Follow up until you have confirmed that your purchase has been recorded.
- Once the deal is done, change the locks on the property immediately. Who knows who might otherwise have a key to the home?

Chapter 14

HOW TO AVOID THE MOST COMMON MISTAKES INVESTORS MAKE

Anybody can receive information; it is the wise man that prospers by it and puts it to use.

—Jeff Adams

As I've emphasized throughout this book, successful REO buying and selling doesn't have to be difficult or confounding. As with most other business endeavors, though, it does come with its share of glitches, bumps, and pitfalls that can threaten to derail a deal or a career. It has its nightmare scenarios, too. The way to get past the roadblocks is to know what to expect, be prepared, and do everything possible to steer around the problems ahead of time.

That doesn't mean you won't make any mistakes. We all do. I've talked about many of mine throughout these pages. The key is to learn from those mistakes and not repeat them. Remember that Zack Childress, an instructor at the Jeff Adams Foreclosure Academy, made a mistake on a rehab that cost him $100,000. But that didn't stop him. Why? Because, he says, if he had done it right, he would have made $200,000 on the property!

In today's economy especially, if you plan for the unexpected and make the right deals when you purchase a property, you can profit no matter the external market forces.

BEYOND YOUR MARKET

It's not enough to know only your market. A savvy investor also needs to have his or her finger on the pulse of real estate markets, the real estate industry, and the economy in general. Economic conditions, after all, affect the availability of your buyers and renters as well as the efficacy of a particular exit strategy. That's one more reason why deals should be geared not to the profit made in selling a property but in buying it instead. Gearing profit toward the front end of a deal builds in insulation against market ups and downs as well as other external forces we can't control.

Importance of Flexibility

Realistically, however, as investors we sometimes do get caught off guard. That's not an excuse for ignoring impending signs of market shifts. But it is an inevitability nonetheless. What's essential is that if the market collapses and you're caught holding a property you had intended to flip, you're flexible enough to switch exit strategies. Hold the property as a rental instead. Then, as markets turn around and equity builds in the property, sell it. By that time, however, you may have decided that holding it as a rental has long-term advantages.

Better still, as you get more familiar and comfortable with REO investing, gear your exit strategy to current market conditions. That means if prices on properties are very low—as they are today—buy and hold as rentals as many as you can, making sure you have positive cash flow. Then, as prices appreciate and equity in the properties build, sell some of those properties to pay off others.

Florida Realtor and real estate investor Alex Galitsky takes this flexibility a step further by diversifying his exit strategies to create multiple income streams to protect his business when the market changes. Galitsky helps other investors buy some properties quickly for smaller commissions; buys, fixes, and flips other properties, usually for higher profits; and then also buys properties and holds them as rentals for cash flow and appreciation.

Tracking the Economy

Many websites provide a quick study of markets and the economy. Several include Inman News (www.inman.com), RealtyTrac (www.realtytrac.com), Realty Times (www.realtytimes.com), HousingWire.com (www.housingwire.com), RISMedia (www.rismedia.com), Mortgage Bankers Association (www.mortgagebankers.org), National Association of Realtors (www.realtor.org), and HSH Associates (www.hsh.com). Some sites also offer free newsletters and access to informative press releases.

TITLE ISSUES

With anti-foreclosure sentiment running strong—Congress temporarily halted foreclosures briefly at the end of 2010—and the most recent scandal surrounding the automatic generation of foreclosure documents (robo-signing), some wonder whether banks really do have clear title to many of REO properties in their portfolios.

MERS Fiasco

Do banks really have clear title to REOs? That question may not be fully answerable, according to Keith Gumbinger, with HSH Associates (www.hsh.com), a New Jersey-based company that tracks mortgages and consumer loan information. Gumbinger has been tracking the industry for more than two decades. He notes that the problem in part stems from the fact that the mortgages on many properties and the foreclosures on them were conducted through Mortgage Electronic Registration Systems (MERS). MERS (www.mersinc.org) is a Reston, Virginia-based private company set up by banks and lenders as an electronic database to keep track of mortgages in order to streamline the process of securitization of mortgages (packaging and keeping them for sale). MERS, an assignee of the lender of record, initiated foreclosure proceedings against thousands of properties as a proxy for the lender, and in a number of cases homeowners have come back to challenge the legality of the process.

It's not clear whether MERS has standing under the statutes in the given states, says Gumbinger. Courts in various states have ruled both ways on the issue. Courts in California, Massachusetts, and Kansas, among other states, have determined that MERS has legal standing; a New York court has ruled that it doesn't. Additionally, MERS has been accused of shoddy business practices and investigated by attorneys general in various states.

The issues and cases are far from over. In February 2011, MERS announced it would propose an amendment to its membership rules that would require member banks and lenders to no longer foreclose on a property in MERS's name (www.mersinc.org/news/details.aspx?id=288).

"If a foreclosure happened outside the boundaries of the law, could a former owner of a home have a claim against the title? I don't know that anyone has an answer to that," says Gumbinger. "Presumably if a lender has made a property available as an REO, it has acquired that property under legal auspices and there are no claims against it when it is sold."

As investors, this is one more issue we all need to be aware of. It doesn't mean we sit on the sidelines when we could be taking advantage of the REO bargains. At the same time, however, if in doing your due diligence you find out that the former property owner plans to sue the mortgage company, steer clear of the deal no matter how attractive it seems.

FORGET THE TAPE MEASURE

Details count in this business, but *not* when it comes to your first look at a property to determine if it's worth an offer. When you're doing a quick first inspection with your real estate agent, forget the minutiae in the house. Guesstimate, and do it quickly. At most take 5 or 10 minutes to get an idea if a property is in good shape, not so good shape, or terrible shape.

Rookie investors with agent in tow will inspect a house with tape measure in hand, taking pictures as they go. Don't make it hard for your agent. Do a quick look; make a fast assessment of the amount of work needed, and then move on to the next property. If the property is a rehab, you'll have the opportunity to see it later with a contractor.

It has been said that experience is the best teacher, although I've come to realize that if I don't try to reinvent the wheel I become successful much faster. I've learned to learn from those who already have achieved what I hope to achieve.

INTERSTATE DEALINGS

Some REO investors opt to do business across state lines—either as an absentee investor or because a metropolitan area may include multiple states. Whatever the reason for interstate buying and selling of

REOs, the most important thing is to know the real estate laws of any state where you're doing business.

If you live in New York and you're buying a property in New Jersey, you need to know New Jersey real estate law, too. A transaction is subject to the laws in the state where the transaction occurs, not necessarily the state where the buyer or seller resides. You also will need the official New Jersey state contract to use in presenting offers on REOs in New Jersey.

SCAM ALERT

As with buying and selling in general, the old saying "caveat emptor" (let the buyer beware) applies when it comes to REOs. If a guru wants your money before demonstrating that his or her system works, dig deeper to ensure you don't fall prey to a scam. If a would-be hard-money lender wants money up front to loan you money, caveat emptor.

Beware the Source Crying Foul

For a sampling of REO-related scams, Google "REO" and "scam." You'll get tens of thousands of hits. A note of caution, however: Make sure whoever is pointing the finger and saying "Scam!" is not a disgruntled homeowner or business partner hoping to get even by bad-mouthing a person or program. Keep in mind that the Internet is not edited for accuracy.

Fake Title Company Scam

One prevalent scam involves REO "wholesalers" who try to flip properties they don't own to legitimate investors. The investors are told to wire the money for a property to the "wholesaler's" title company—it's fake—and then they're gone.

To avoid being snared by this scam, when purchasing an REO deal from another investor, always use your own reputable title company, and make sure you have a free and clear title policy for a property *before* wiring any cash.

DON'T FORGET TO SELL

Many investors make the mistake of only buying real estate at great prices and then forget about the importance of selling properties. These investors are rightly taking care of tomorrow's cash flow needs by buying now. But in the process they overextend themselves financially because they overlook their cash flow needs today.

The best strategy for financial security today and tomorrow is to buy *and sell* REOs. As I suggested earlier in the book, consider holding for rental one of every four properties you purchase. Then, over a period of five to seven years, after you've amassed a sizable portfolio and property values have appreciated, sell half the properties and use the proceeds to pay off the loans on the other half. You're then left owning properties free and clear that can provide a steady revenue stream.

TOP MISTAKES REAL ESTATE INVESTORS MAKE

Successful real estate investing is about watching and learning from others, then adapting what you have learned to your needs and doing it better. That's another reason networking is so important in this business. Find out what mistakes others have made, and don't make them yourself. Here are some of the most-often-mentioned mistakes that now-successful real estate investors say they have made. They're not necessarily specific only to REO investing, and they can be applied to real estate investing in general. Not one of the issues, however, proved so much of a problem or obstacle that an investor gave up on his or her promising investing career. All are manageable, as we've talked about throughout this book:

- Waiting too long to begin investing in real estate.
- Not having a plan.
- Not requiring written repair bids every time.
- Not charging for tenant damage to a property.
- Not screening tenants for eviction risks.
- Paying for repairs or construction before 100 percent completion.
- Paying full price for late repair or construction.

- Allowing your real estate business to run your life.
- Overimproving a property purchased to flip or rent.
- Running out of cash.
- Forgetting about asset protection.
- Overanalyzing a property.
- Becoming friends with tenants.
- Underinsuring property and risk.
- Ignoring cash flow.
- Punishing bad tenants without rewarding good ones.
- Permitting tenants' problems to spoil the positives of real estate investment.
- Allowing rent collections to get personal.
- Taking the time to personally see a property *only* when there is a problem.
- Not thinking of tenants as potential buyers.
- Renting to relatives.

Now it's your turn to heed the advice and experiences of others, anticipate the issues before they arise, and make contingency plans to handle them.

Part III

EXIT STRATEGIES

WHOLESALE YOUR PROPERTY TO ANOTHER INVESTOR

Chapter 15

WHOLESALE YOUR PROPERTY TO ANOTHER INVESTOR

Start with wholesaling properties because it's the most risk-free way to invest in real estate.
          —**Gerald Lucas, real estate coach, mentor, and author**

Buying an REO and flipping it wholesale to another investor is quick and painless, and it doesn't take any of your own money. It also is a great way for a beginner to learn how to evaluate properties while building investing experience and capital. You risk almost nothing but your time!

Wholesaling properties isn't only for beginners, either. Brian Holmes is a former stockbroker turned real estate investor, and an instructor with the Jeff Adams Foreclosure Academy. "We wholesale everything," he says. As a wholesaler, Holmes buys real estate at a reduced price, then acts as a middleman and flips it to someone (an investor) who in turn will often repair the property and resell it at retail or hold it as a rental.

Wholesaling REO properties to other investors is the fastest way to build capital. The paycheck for each deal usually is an acquisition or flipping fee—a few thousand dollars and up. Because the entire transaction can be relatively quick and involves none of your own money, the risk is minimal and the payoff swift and worthwhile. Remember Alex Galitsky, the Florida REO agent and real estate investor who helps investors pick up properties for a finder's fee as little as $1,000 per property? It takes him only a few minutes to fill out the paperwork, and his investors in turn pay him a quick $1,000 to $5,000—not bad wages for a few minutes' time!

THE IMPORTANCE OF MARKET VALUE

Forget how much you think someone should pay you for a property. Without the numbers to back it up, that amount is pointless. One of the biggest problems confronting many REO investors, no matter their exit strategy, is that they don't know how to determine the market value of a property. Figuring those numbers can be daunting, but—as with most other real estate number-crunching—plenty of help is available. The professionals on your power team who know and understand the numbers should be your primary source. (See the Addendum at the end of this book for more on deciphering the numbers.)

We talked about valuation of properties in Chapter 11, but it's worth reviewing here because the numbers are so important in determining an exit strategy. Basically, a property's market value is what the property will sell for in a reasonable period of time. Market value depends on the condition of the property and how it stacks up against similar properties in the same area.

To determine market value requires a comparative market analysis, which can come from your real estate agent, and should include at least two comps from different sources like a title company and the MLS. Another option is to check listings for similar properties on websites like Redfin (www.redfin.com) and Realtor.com (www.realtor.com), as long as those listings are within at most the last 90 days. Be sure to see the comparable properties in person, too, to make sure the properties really are similar. If you're still unsure as to how your property stacks up against the competition, contact top agents in the market and ask their advice.

FINDING YOUR BUYERS: CASH BUYER LISTS

Many of my properties sell before they're ever repaired because I have worked hard to put together a wholesale buyers list. All your networking can and does pay off, especially when it comes to flipping properties. In both of the following scenarios, a reliable buyers list turned what could have been nonexistent deals into successful moneymakers.

Because I have an extensive buyers list, when a property comes on the market, I'll typically call three or four of the most consistent wholesale buyers on my list to tell them I have a property that might interest them. I'll let them know the property's address, the after-repair value (ARV), and my selling price. I do *not* tell them my purchase price. It's then up to the potential buyer to decide if he or she wants to look into the deal further.

I begin something like this:

Hi, this is Jeff Adams. I have a home at 123 Any Street in Any-where, USA, that I think might interest you. It's worth $100,000, and I'm selling it for $67,000. By the way, I also gave the address to three other investors, so get back to me as soon as possible if you're interested, okay?

Most of these wholesale buyers get back to me right away.

PROFIT IS PROFIT

Not every property that an investor flips wholesale has to net huge profits. As an investor, don't shy away from good properties with profit potential. Less room for profit may demand more creative approaches to a deal, but profits are there nonetheless. After all, if you don't play the game, you don't have a chance to win. Not every deal will be a home run, but singles and doubles add up.

For example, assume that an REO with an ARV of $100,000 is sell-ing for $65,000. What if an investor knew she had a buyer on her list who unequivocally would jump on the property immediately at 70 cents on the dollar because the property is located in a solid area where the buyer already has rental properties? The investor could seal the deal for $65,000, then call her wholesale buyer with the deal and flip it for a quick profit of $5,000. This is a situation in which transac-tional funding might be used. That's when the wholesaler uses some-one else's funds for a very short period of time—perhaps 24 to 48 hours—to make the deal, and in that time flips the property to another investor.

CASH BUYERS LISTS

Plenty of people and organizations tout "cash buyers lists," which con-tain the names and supposed contact information of individuals and groups reportedly ready and willing to pay cash for properties. Google "cash buyers list" and you'll get thousands of hits. Keep in mind, though, that not all lists of supposed investors are created equal. The quality of a list—its reliability and accuracy—depends on its source.

Build Your Own

Work at building your own cash buyers list. It's likely to be more reliable in the long run. That's what I did, and the effort has paid off many times over.

Some ways to build your list include:

- **Contact other investors in your market.** Earlier we talked about your competitors as your potential buyers, whether they are competing against you at auctions and/or on deals through REO agents.
- **Find cash buyers in your market.** Ask title companies for a list of all the transactions that have closed in your area in the past year. Properties purchased without a new loan and by an absentee owner are cash transactions, and those owners represent potential cash buyers.
- **Contact local investor clubs.** Go to the meetings and network. Stand up, introduce yourself, and present your property for wholesale.
- **Check websites and local media.** Search advertisements containing "I buy homes," "cash for homes," and other related keywords. Some national websites to visit include MyHouseDeals. com (www.myhousedeals.com), RehabList (www.rehablist. com), Craigslist (www.craigslist.com), backpage.com (www. backpage.com), and Trulia (www.trulia.com).

FINDING YOUR BUYERS II: ALL THE RIGHT MOVES

Just as you build your cash buyers list step by step, build your marketing efforts, too. My strategies call for driving traffic to my website where I showcase homes for sale at wholesale.

Among the other steps I take to find wholesale buyers for properties:

- Place ads on other websites.
- Place ads in the local newspapers.

- Look for a potential buyer at the "We Buy Houses" ads in the newspaper.
- Network with other investors, including local real estate investment clubs.
- Network with top real estate agents. They generally know of buyers and sellers. A quick way to do this is by blast-faxing them a one-page marketing piece on the particular property or properties.

My Whole-Tailing Strategy

One of my all-time favorite exit strategies that I learned from my colleague Mike Cantu is what I call whole-tailing—a combination of wholesaling and retailing. An investor buys a property, does minimal but very visual cleanup on the exterior of the property, and then lists it back on the MLS a week or so later at a higher (but still wholesale) price and with the caveats "needs interior carpet and paint."

Minimal cleanup involves hauling away the trash (exterior and interior), painting the exterior, and adding some landscaping such as planting flowers and greening the lawn. The interior isn't repaired, but the investor has spent very little money on the property. Once people see the property and like its curb appeal, they go inside and often decide they can rework the interior themselves. First-time homebuyers are happy to put in the extra effort in exchange for the discount on the price.

For example, I pay $60,000 for a house with an ARV of $100,000. My crew comes in and for a few thousand dollars does a quick and simple cleanup of the exterior. A week later, I relist the house on the MLS for $85,000. Even after paying my cleanup crew and for the paint and supplies, my profit for the week's work is $10,000 to $15,000, and the price of the house is still well below the home's market value. It's a win-win for buyer and seller.

Showing the Property

When a property is being flipped at wholesale, it's not necessary to show the property to everyone who calls. When people express interest in a property, give them the address so they can see it themselves. If after driving by or walking around the exterior of the property they call you back, you can make arrangements to show the property. I usually put lockboxes on my properties to allow my wholesale buyers easy access to them. Lockboxes are available relatively inexpensively at home improvement stores.

Additionally, holding an open house for several hours on a Saturday will allow a number of people to see the property.

Whenever someone tours a property, make sure to have a sign-in sheet that includes space for contact information. That's one more way to build your buyers list.

Chapter 16

FIXING UP AND SELLING THE PROPERTY AT RETAIL

First-time homebuyers are one of the best target markets.
— Jeff Adams

A fast-track investor's approach to creating long-term wealth from REOs is to buy and sell several properties each year, and then use the profits to pay off mortgages on other properties fast. Instead of flipping properties for more and more purchases, you're using the proceeds to pay down your loans. With this strategy, you are generating current income and guaranteeing free and clear rental properties in the near future. We talk more about this strategy in Chapter 17.

When it comes to marketing and selling my properties, I like to think outside the box and beyond the typical approach my competition is likely to take. You can use such thinking as one more opportunity to differentiate yourself and walk away a winner. A huge part of being a successful REO investor is staying ahead of the competition by attracting buyers and leveraging all the tools available, including the Internet and other technologies. But that doesn't mean that I overlook tried-and-true traditional approaches.

The day I close on a property that I want to flip to a retail homebuyer, I put a big banner on the property and a sign in the yard that reads, "Own This Home for $500 Down," and I include my website and contact information. I also take out advertisements in the local newspaper and feature the property on my website.

With this guerrilla marketing strategy, I generate neighborhood buzz, interest in the property, and possible interest from others who know people looking to buy a home. Often the home sells before it's ever repaired, saving me thousands of dollars in real estate sales commissions. The strategy also drives traffic to my website, where I collect contact information for my prospective buyers', tenants', and sellers' lists. All of the above is essential to power an ongoing successful real estate investment business that counts on buying and flipping or renting properties.

SELL TO FIRST-TIME HOMEBUYERS WHO QUALIFY FOR FHA LOANS

My target audience for many of the homes I flip is first-time homebuyers who can qualify for the federal government's Federal Housing Administration (FHA) loan program (www.hud.gov/buying/loans. cfm). The FHA grants loans to individuals with good credit and requires only 3 percent down on a property purchase. The FHA also has a gift program that allows a relative to gift the 3 percent down payment. We pay the other 3 percent in closing costs. As an added bonus for a potential buyer and seller/investor, the FHA even has loans that allow a buyer to fold repair costs into one loan.

I get my property sold with a comfortable profit, and a family gets a new home at a bargain price. Again, this is a win-win situation for both parties—buyer and seller.

MARKETING TACTICS TO GENERATE BUYERS

Which approach should you use to sell your property? If you're a proactive investor looking to generate deals and more deals, market your property in every way possible. Real estate investors often make the mistake of relying on only one or two forms of marketing. To find and move properties, use whatever means are available and necessary.

Many of the marketing tactics that work to attract wholesale buyers also work with retail ones. That includes networking with other investors, real estate agents, and title companies; aggressively advertising the property "For Sale by Owner" on websites, in newspapers, and other local publications; and blast-faxing flyers on a property to real estate agents. Don't overlook real estate investment club meetings, either, as a way to get the word out about your property.

MLS Listing Service

Another good way to find buyers for a property is by listing it on the MLS. An investor can pay a flat MLS listing fee—$300 to $350—and then simply pay a commission to the selling agent who delivers the offer.

One way I stay ahead of the competition is to offer the agent who brings me a full-price offer a full 5 to 6 percent commission. Typically the standard 6 percent commission is split between the buyer's agent and the seller's agent. By offering the selling agent the full commission, I create further incentive for the agent to sell my property first.

Other Flat-Fee Listing Services

A number of other websites tout flat-fee listings, but do your due diligence before shelling out any money to list a property. Make sure the site is current and well respected, and that it gets heavy traffic. To find some alternative listing sites, Google "flat-fee listing" and "real estate."

Build in the Right Strategies

Pay attention to the nuances that can make marketing a property more successful:

- **Categories.** When running a newspaper ad, use the classified categories "Homes for Sale" and "Homes for Rent."
- **Timeliness.** When running a newspaper ad, choose Sundays (generally the largest circulation day). However, avoid holiday weekends unless they are in conjunction with a big sporting event like the Super Bowl. People tend not to read newspapers on those weekends.
- **Content.** In web ads as well as newspapers and periodicals, use catchy titles—"own this home for $500 down," for example.
- **Signs.** Try posting signs where it's legal.

REPAIRING A PROPERTY

As you read earlier, when repairing an REO to flip at retail, remember that it isn't about installing the latest and greatest of everything. After all, the money you spend to repair a property comes out of your pocket. Do the minimum required to bring the property up to code and to the standards set by comparable properties in the neighborhood. But do just enough extra so that your property is just a little bit better, a little nicer than the competition. New paint and new carpet or flooring are usually standard parts of repair.

Pay attention to the property's curb appeal, too. A green lawn and a few flowers will go a long way toward generating interest in a property, especially among first-time homebuyers. If you're uncertain whether a new exterior paint job and front door are enough to boost your property's curb appeal, drive around and look at the competition. Which properties look the most inviting? Make sure your property looks a little bit better and is priced better, too.

If you have a rehabber or contractor on your team, make sure he or she understands the importance of keeping repairs, costs, and the time involved to a minimum. Time is money. Any delays in flipping the property and cashing your profit check can be costly down the road.

SHOWING A PROPERTY

When you are trying to sell or rent a property, it makes sense to show it yourself. Why pay your real estate agent or assistant unless you have multiple showings at the same time? You don't have to be an expert or even especially gregarious to show a property, but you do have to use some common sense.

Whether you are holding an open house or a private showing, try to look at the property through the prospective buyer's or renter's eyes, emphasizing the positives and minimizing any drawbacks. Draw attention to the nice windows—and not the small closet—in the second bedroom; point out any special architectural features like arched doorways or built-in bookcases rather than the dated bathroom (which did not need an expensive remodel). If the prospect has children, a big backyard is a plus even if it's not beautifully landscaped. For a retired couple, a small yard may be appealing because of its minimum maintenance.

Whenever you show a property, try to arrive a half hour early to pop some break-and-bake or other premade cookies into the oven. Not only will the aroma create a homey atmosphere, but prospects will spend a little more time at your property to eat the cookies, and they will leave with an added favorable impression.

In the time it takes for the cookies to bake, do a last-minute inspection—picking up any trash that may have blown into the yard, for instance. You also might want to do some minimal staging. A couple of plants and a lightweight wicker chair and table, for example, can add warm touches to an empty house. You can keep a box of props ready to go for whenever you have a showing.

You want to put your best foot forward in every phase of selling a property. And you get only one chance to make a first impression.

Chapter 17

BUYING AND HOLDING: RENTING THE PROPERTY FOR A POSITIVE MONTHLY CASH FLOW

This is your business. Don't allow rent collection to get personal.
— Jeff Adams

Years ago, I asked one of my mentors in this business why he didn't buy and hold properties as rentals. His response: "Why do I want to be broke (cash flow-wise) managing all those rental properties?"

The problem, of course, wasn't with the buy, hold, and rent strategy. It was that my mentor felt a long-term strategy wouldn't leave him with adequate cash flow in the short term. I've found that buying REOs at reduced prices and holding them as rentals is an excellent strategy that allows an investor to take care of future cash flow needs. However, as an investor, it's important to also take care of today's cash flow needs by buying, fixing up, and flipping some of those properties for immediate profits. Better yet, as an REO investor who can buy properties for pennies on the dollar, why not keep one of every four houses you purchase, build your portfolio, and retire with riches!

If that sounds appealing, make sure to choose properties with good cash flow—nice older homes in good neighborhoods, usually three-bedroom/two-bath, or even two-bedroom/one-bath properties. In five years, you'll end up with a portfolio of 20 homes. When the market comes back, sell half and pay off the mortgages on the rest. That's possible because, remember, the properties initially were purchased well below their after-repair value (ARV). Recently I bought an REO on Moffit Avenue in Rialto, California, for $155,000. The property has a current ARV of $240,000, while three years ago the same property was valued at $400,000. I decided to keep it as a rental because it's in a great neighborhood, close to schools, and has a positive cash flow of more than $700 a month. My strategy calls for putting that extra money toward paying off the property's mortgage as soon as possible because I want to take care of tomorrow's cash flow needs.

Generally speaking, buying a property to hold and rent for monthly income is a more advanced exit strategy than simply picking up an REO property and flipping it. That doesn't mean it can't be done by new investors. It simply means the investor must be thorough and careful in all aspects of the deal and understand the nuances of being a landlord.

Let's take a closer look.

WHEN BUY, HOLD, AND RENT CAN MAKE SENSE

Whether or not you decide to try my hold-one-of-four approach, some economic and market circumstances favor buying an REO to hold for rental as the best, most economically advantageous exit strategy. In other cases, no matter the state of the real estate market, an REO investor may set out to find income-producing rental properties. Earlier in the book I mentioned Eugene Seagriff, who did just that when he bought a four-unit property in Phillipsburg, New Jersey. Seagriff has a full-time job and invests in real estate part-time.

If you do plan to hold a property that was purchased initially with a hard-money loan, after the deal closes, you need to wait (usually about six months) for the loan to season—to prove to the lender you can pay the mortgage—before refinancing for a long-term, better-rate loan on the property. That's where relationships with a bank or mortgage lender on your power team can really smooth the process.

Every investor's circumstances differ, just as each person's goals differ. Following are some reasons and situations in which holding a property as a rental could make the most investing sense.

For Monthly Cash Flow

Whether or not immediate cash flow is an investor's top priority, it can make sense to hold on to an REO after purchase to use as a rental until property prices appreciate. Real estate is one of the few investments that you can buy for little money down and that pays for itself over time. If you can afford to keep a property as a rental, it can be an excellent addition to your portfolio and provide regular monthly income.

Remember New York attorney Teresa R. Martin in Chapter 1? She purchased an REO triplex that provides her with an extra $1,000 a month in income.

If You Have Trouble Selling a Property

Sometimes, no matter how well a property is priced, it simply doesn't sell. It could be the market; the location may not be as strong as your research initially indicated, or the area may be suffering an economic decline of some type. The loss or significant downsizing of a major employer, for example, can cripple a community and wreak havoc on local real estate. That's what happened over the past several years in areas like Detroit, Michigan, where troubled U.S. automakers laid off thousands of workers and many homeowners simply walked away from their homes.

If selling the property at below-market value is not an option, renting it may be a positive cash-flow alternative.

If Property Is Vacant or Already Rented

Many REO properties are vacant when they're acquired. If you don't already have a buyer lined up, sometimes it's less hassle and headache to rent the property instead of trying to sell it. It's also less expensive initially to rent out the property because a rental may only require some cosmetic repairs—paint and new carpet, for example—as opposed to a full rehab if the property were to be sold.

Also, if an REO acquisition already is rented—for example, you acquire a duplex, a triplex, or some other larger REO—as the buyer you're usually required to honor the existing leases. In that case it's a no-brainer—your REO comes with instant cash flow already in place, so enjoy it and cash those monthly checks.

However, a word of advice: Be careful of the tenants who come with the property. They're not always top-notch. Eugene Seagriff can attest to that: "On the positive side, when I bought my four-unit property I negotiated aggressively to get the best price I could. Originally the quadplex was priced at $390,000, and I bought it for $305,000. But one of the things I did wrong was allow the seller to fill some of the vacancies while we were in negotiations. They weren't good tenants. I ended up evicting them pretty soon after the deal closed."

SCREEN TENANTS

Always screen tenants! That includes running background checks to determine if someone has a police record and decent credit. I rent my properties to only 1 of every 10 people who apply—that's 10 percent of the applicants. It pays to be choosy—my tenants pay on time and take pride in (and take care of) their rental homes.

Looks Can Be Deceiving

I have had my own tenant nightmares, including threats of bodily harm. When I first starting buying and renting properties, I didn't bother to take the time to qualify or screen renters. I learned the hard way.

One day my agent brought in a well-dressed man as a potential tenant for a property I had recently purchased. The potential tenant seemed nice, so I agreed to rent to him. He gave me a check for the deposit and first month's rent. The check bounced, so I went back to him and he gave me another check. That one bounced, too. By the time I went to see the tenant after the second bounced check, I was mad. When he invited me into the house—the house I owned—he pulled a gun on me. I was able to talk my way out of the situation, but it took me three months to get the tenant, who had never paid me a dime, evicted. Screen your tenants, period.

Tenant Successes

Not all tenants, of course, are of the nightmare variety. Some people voluntarily choose to rent or simply don't have a down payment for a house. They always pay on time, are very gracious and appreciative, and take care of the property.

With today's tsunami of foreclosures, many people end up losing their homes and have no choice but to rent. They, too, pay their bills; they just got in over their heads and can't afford a mortgage right now. I have had success with such renters.

Screening Is Worth the Time and Money

Screening tenants can be a lot of work, especially if you have multiple properties. But the alternative can be far worse. Either properly manage the property yourself or hire a management company, which also can be a big help when it comes to filling vacancies. If you have a large number of properties, a management company almost always is a must.

One way to cut out some of the work is by offering your good tenants incentives to handle minor repairs and problems themselves. If, for example, the going rental rate on a property is $1,500 a month, offer the property for $1,400 a month with the stipulation that the tenant will handle the first $50 in repairs. That way your tenants are less likely to hound you as the landlord for minor problems like leaky faucets or overflowing toilets.

MORE TENANT WISDOM

Entire books have been written on how to be a landlord. However, the most important rule to keep in mind is: This is your business. Do not allow yourself to get emotionally involved. This is your livelihood. Don't forget it.

Some other helpful tips to help improve your experiences as a landlord:

- A bad tenant can take several months to evict—in some places much longer. Adding to the headache, the tenant may trash the property during that time. I'll say it one more time: Screen your tenants!

- Don't punish the bad tenants and forget the good ones. Reward the good tenants, and watch your tenant turnover rate drop. If your tenants have paid the rent on time for a year, consider showing some appreciation. You might give them a turkey for Thanksgiving, offer to paint a room, offer to put new carpet in one of the rooms, or even hand out ice-cream-cone gift certificates in the summer. The cost of turning over a unit is much greater than any of these small expenses, and the rewards of keeping a good tenant far outweigh any extra cost.

- Set rules for your tenants. If you don't, you'll burn out in the business as a result of tenant headaches, and there can be plenty.
- When setting rents, contact property management companies, check local classified ads, and do other homework to determine rents on comparable properties.

BUILDING YOUR PROSPECTIVE TENANTS' LIST

Just as you build a buyers list or an REO agents list, I recommend you build a prospective tenants list, too, so that in the event one tenant moves out you have another waiting in the wings to move right in. Make sure you have a systematic way to capture phone numbers, e-mail addresses, and other contact information for potential tenants.

You may want to list the property for rent on the MLS. You can do that through the real estate agent on your power team. Neighborhood referrals and a Saturday open house are other strategies that often work well. Word of mouth is another powerful referral service, and often can lead to quality tenants.

Some other ways to attract potential tenants include:

- Ads on websites like Craigslist (www.craigslist.com), Trulia (www.trulia.com), and backpage.com (www.backpage.com).
- A sign or banner outside the property that says "For Rent by Owner." Include your phone number and website address.
- Classified advertisements online in local newspapers, and in other local sources.
- Property management companies.
- Rental agencies. Some have no or minimal fees. Look for the agency with the most signs in your area and at the least call them to find out more.

UNDERSTANDING BUYING FORMULAS

Whether you're a new or an experienced investor, it's crucial to be able to calculate the cash flow on a property to ascertain whether it's a good deal. Following is a brief look at how to determine certain numbers essential to an investor's success equation.

CASH FLOW ANALYSIS

Cash flow is the amount left over after all expenses have been paid and mortgage payments, if any, have been made. Investors often use the 1 percent rule when evaluating income-producing properties: You must generate at least 1 percent of the purchase price in monthly income. For example, if you buy a house for $100,000, your cash flow should be at least $1,000 a month.

This scenario works well with traditional financing on a property with a typical down payment of 20 percent to 30 percent of the purchase price.

- Step 1: Determine the property's monthly rent. If the property is already rented, that step has been done for you. Otherwise, look at ads for comparable properties; you can call regarding those ads and pose as a tenant looking for a property to rent. (For our example, assume the rent is $600 per month.)
- Step 2: Multiply the monthly rental amount by 12 (months) to calculate the yearly rental income on the property.
- Step 3: Calculate the vacancy allowance. In a strong rental market, it's 4 percent to 5 percent. Now subtract that amount from the annual income to calculate the gross operating income. This is the actual amount of money that will pass through your hands.
- Step 4: Subtract all of the operating expenses from the gross operating income to calculate your net operating income (NOI). Operating expenses include property taxes, property insurance, maintenance, repair costs, utilities included with the tenant's rent, advertising, accounting, and management fees.

Example:

$$\text{Gross operating income} = (\text{Monthly rental income} \times 12 \text{ months}) - \text{Vacancy allowance}$$

or

$$\text{Gross operating income} = (\$600 \times 12) - \$360 = \$6,840$$

$$\text{Net operating income} = \text{gross operating income} - \text{operating expenses}$$

or

$$\text{Net operating income} = \$6,840 - \$2,052 = \$4,788$$

For a single-family home, operating expenses typically run between 25 percent and 30 percent of the gross income figure. The net operating income is the amount of money available to pay the mortgage on the property (or debt service). If debt service is in the negative, you should restructure the mortgage payment, pay less for the property, increase the rents, or lower the expenses. The bottom line is indicative of how much debt a property will support. After subtracting the mortgage payment, the final cash flow is what's left.

CAPITALIZATION RATE

Capitalization rate or cap rate is the ratio of net operating income (NOI) divided by the sales price of the property, and can be used to help define the estimated value of income-producing properties. The next example assumes an NOI of $12,000.

Example:

$$\text{NOI/Sales price} = \text{Cap rate}$$

or

$$\$12,000/\$200,000 = 6\%$$

Most investors have a preferred cap rate they require for an investment. If you already know the net operating income, simply divide it by the desired cap rate to calculate the price you're willing to pay for the property.

Example:

$$\$12,000/6\% = \$200,000$$

The primary advantage of a cap rate is that it provides a quick overview of the financial reliability of an investment. Its main drawback, though, is that it takes into consideration only the relationship between the property's net operating income and its purchase price (or value). Investors typically finance a portion of the purchase price with mortgage financing. Interest on borrowed funds, income taxes, and capital improvements aren't usually considered operating expenses, and are exclusive to each investor's equity investment and tax circumstances.

The cap rate doesn't automatically become your return on investment, and the NOI isn't automatically considered your before-tax cash. But consider the scenario in which you pay cash for a property. In this case, your NOI is equal to your before-tax cash flow, and the cap rate is equal to your before-tax cash.

Example:

A $1,000,000 property with an NOI of $100,000 has a cap rate of 10 percent.

If an investor requires a 12 percent cap rate for the investment, how much would the investor pay for the property?

Answer: NOI of $100,000/12% = $833,333.33

Sources of capitalization rate data include appraisers, lenders, and recent sales of comparable properties in the area. If reliable cap rate data are not available, use the following calculations to estimate the prices for similar income properties.

$$\text{Cap rate} = \text{NOI/Value}$$

$$\text{Estimated market value} = \text{NOI/Cap rate}$$

Example:

A property has an NOI of $100,000 and the asking price is $1,000,000.

$$\text{Cap rate} = \$100,000/\$1,000,000 \times 100 = 10\%$$

Example:

A property has an NOI of $120,000, and the cap rates for similar properties in the same area are 12 %

Estimated market value = $120,000/12% = $1,000,000

Got that? If not, don't worry. Again, there are plenty of online calculators, cell-phone applications you can download, and other electronic options to help you and your power team deal with the numbers.

CASH-ON-CASH RETURN

Cash-on-cash return is a percentage that measures the return on cash invested in an income-producing property and is a useful tool for comparing investment properties. Cash-on-cash return is calculated by dividing the before-tax cash flow by the amount of cash invested, and then it's expressed as a percentage.

Example:

If the before-tax cash flow for an investment property is $20,000 and the amount of cash invested in the property is $120,000, the cash-on-cash return is 16.67 percent.

$$\text{Cash-on-cash return} = \text{Before-tax cash flow}/\text{Cash invested} \times 100$$

or

$$\text{Cash-on-cash return} = \$20,000/\$120,000 \times 100 = 16.67\%$$

DEBT SERVICE COVERAGE RATIO

The debt service coverage ratio (DSCR) measures an income-producing property's ability to cover the mortgage payments. It's calculated by dividing the net operating income (NOI) by the annual debt service.

Annual debt service is equal to the annual total of all interest and principal paid for all the loans on a property. For example, a debt service coverage ratio less than 1 indicates the income property doesn't generate enough cash flow to cover the mortgage payments. A DSCR of 0.9 indicates negative cash flow and that the income covers only 90 percent of the annual mortgage payments or debt service on the property.

In contrast, a property with a DSCR of 1.25 generates 1.25 times as much annual income as the annual debt service on the property.

Example:

> You want to buy an investment property with a net operating income of $24,000 and an annual debt service of $20,000.
>
> DSCR = NOI/Annual debt service = $24,000/$20,000 = 1.2
>
> That means the property generates 20 percent more annual income than is required to cover the annual mortgage payments.

Most lending institutions require a minimum debt coverage ratio value in order to make a loan on income-producing properties. Typically, debt service coverage ratio requirements for lending institutions range between 1.1 and 1.35.

GROSS RENT MULTIPLIER

The gross rent multiplier (GRM) is a ratio and another way to estimate the value of income-producing properties. The average GRM of similar properties in an area can also estimate the value of other like properties.

The monthly or yearly GRM is calculated by dividing the sales price by the monthly or yearly potential gross income.

Example:

> If the sales price for a property is $150,000 and the property's monthly potential gross income is $2,000, the monthly GRM is equal to 75.
>
> Gross rent multiplier (monthly) = Sales price/
> Monthly potential gross income
>
> GRM = $150,000/$2,000 = 75

Let's say that as an investor you own several similar properties that sold recently, and their average GRM is 75. You can use this information to estimate the value of comparable properties for sale. For example, if your monthly potential gross income for a property is $3,500, estimate its value as follows:

$$\text{Estimated market value} = \text{GRM} \times \text{Potential gross income}$$

$$\text{Estimated market value} = 75 \times \$3,500 = \$262,500$$

This approach provides only a rough property value estimate. It requires consistent and accurate financial information, and does not include operating expenses, debt service, and taxes. It's possible to have two properties with approximately the same potential gross income, but one has significantly higher operating expenses. The formula also doesn't take into account the vacancy factor.

LOAN TO VALUE

Use loan to value (LTV) to calculate the ratio between the loan balance and the market value of a property expressed as a percent.
Example:

A property with a loan balance of $250,000 and a market value of $350,000 has an LTV of 71 percent.

$$\text{LTV} = \text{Loan balance/Market value} \times 100$$

$$\text{LTV} = \$250,000/\$350,000 \times 100 = 0.71 \times 100 = 71\%$$

Use the LTV to estimate the amount of equity you have in a property. For example, if the LTV for a property is 71 percent, your equity position in the property is 100 percent minus 71 percent, which is 29 percent. You can then multiply 0.29 times the market value to determine the equity amount. So if the market value is $350,000, then the equity amount is $101,500.

GLOSSARY

Absolute auction   An auction at which properties are sold for the highest bid, with no minimum bids established, regardless of price.

Abstract   A summary, as in an abstract of title or judgment.

Abstract of judgment   A summary of a court judgment that creates a lien against a property when filed with the county recorder.

Abstract of title   A summary of the history of ownership (title to) real estate, including original and subsequent conveyances and encumbrances that affect the property as well as abstractor certification that the title history is complete and accurate.

Acceleration clause   The clause in a mortgage or deed of trust that can force immediate payment of the full debt in the event the borrower defaults on an installment payment or other covenant.

Accrued items   Expense items on a closing statement that are incurred but not yet payable, such as taxes on real property.

Addendum   Any addition or change to a contract.

Adjustable rate mortgage (ARM)   A mortgage loan with an interest rate that fluctuates.

Agent   A representative licensed by a particular state to conduct real estate transactions.

Agreement of sale   A signed, written contract between the seller and buyer for sale of real property under specific terms and conditions; also an agreement to convey.

All-inclusive deed of trust   A form of deed of trust that, in addition to any other amounts actually financed, includes the amounts of any prior deeds of trust. Sometimes referred to as a wraparound or overriding trust deed.

Amortization   Repayment of a debt in installments.

Appraisal   An estimate of a property's value made by an independent third party trained to do so.

Appraise   To fix or set a price or value.

Appreciation   The difference between a property's increased value and its original value.

As is   In the current condition. Most properties at auction are sold in their current condition; it's the buyer's responsibility to examine the property.

Assessor   A city or government employee who estimates the value of properties for tax purposes.

Assignment   The method in which a right or contract is transferred from one person to another.

Assumable mortgage   A mortgage that can be taken over by the buyer when a home is sold.

Bank letter of credit   A letter from a bank certifying that a person is worthy of a given level of credit; the same as a proof-of-funds letter required with an REO offer.

Bankruptcy   A filing in federal bankruptcy court to allow a creditor to reorganize or discharge credit obligations due to insolvency.

Beneficiary   An individual entitled to money or assets from a trust or estate. A lender is a beneficiary with a deed of trust or note used to secure a loan.

Bid   An offer by an intending purchaser to pay a designated price for property that is about to be sold at auction.

Bid assistants   Employees of the auctioneer who are usually positioned throughout the crowd of bidders on the auction floor to help the auctioneer spot bidders and to help control and influence the crowd.

Bidding limit   Theoretically, the top price bidders will pay for a property; the limit is self-imposed and set in a bidder's mind.

Bill of sale   A written document by which the title to personal property is transferred from one party to another.

Bird dog   A slang name given to people who bring investors leads to often vacant or run-down properties, generally in exchange for a finder's fee.

Blanket deed of trust   A deed of trust secured by more than one lot or parcel of land.

Breach   The breaking or violating of a law, a right, obligation, engagement, or duty, either by commission or omission.

Broker   An agent authorized by the state to deal in real estate.

Broker's price opinion (BPO)   An estimate of property's market value by a broker, and without a formal appraisal.

Buyback   An item withdrawn from sale because it does not attract the reserve established by the seller.

Buy-down mortgage   A financing technique used to reduce the monthly payments for the first few years of a loan. Funds in the form of discount points are given to the lender by the builder or seller to buy down or lower the effective interest rate paid by the buyer, thus reducing the monthly payments for a set time.

Buyer's market   A market in which there are fewer buyers than sellers.

Buyer's premium   A percentage amount added to the winning bid to be paid by the buyer for the services of the auctioneer.

Capital gain   The profit earned from the sale of an asset.

Cash flow   A surplus left after cash generated from rents is used to pay all operating expenses and mortgage payments.

Certificate of sale   A certificate issued at a judicial sale that entitles the buyer to receive a deed after confirmation of court for the purchase of the property.

Chain of title   A succession of conveyances that make up a title record for a specific parcel of real estate.

Closing costs   Supplementary expenses in the sale of real estate, including loan, title, and appraisal fees.

Closing date   The date set and agreed to on which a buyer takes over a property.

Cloud on title   An outstanding claim that contradicts a title record and can impair (or cloud) the title to a piece of property.

Code   A collection of laws relating to a topic such as real estate.

Co-signer   An individual who signs a promissory note and takes responsibility for the debt.

Collateral   Real estate or personal property pledged as security for a debt.

Comparables   Properties that are similar; used as a comparison to determine a property's market value.

Conditions of sale   The legal terms that govern the conduct of the sale, including acceptable methods of payment, terms, buyer's premiums, and reserve prices.

Contingency   A condition that must be fulfilled before a contract becomes binding.

Contract   An agreement between parties that obligates those parties.

Conventional loan   A loan that requires no insurance or guarantees.

Conveyance   A written instrument that transfers title to or an interest in land from one party to another (for example, a deed, an assignment, a bill of sale).

Counteroffer   A response to an offer.

Credit report   A credit bureau document that gives a credit rating and financial data on a person or company; used by businesses, banks, and others to evaluate credit risk.

Debt ratio   A ratio that compares total monthly payments of a borrower's debts with the borrower's gross monthly income. Also known as debt-to-income ratio.

Deed   A written instrument that, when executed and delivered, conveys title to or an interest in real estate.

Deed in lieu of foreclosure   A situation in which a property owner, with the lender's approval, relinquishes the property to the lender to avoid foreclosure.

Deed of reconveyance   A deed that, when a mortgage is paid in full, releases and discharges a deed of trust.

Deed of trust (trust deed)   A multiparty security agreement that conveys legal title to real property as security for repayment of a loan; the owner is the trustor, a neutral third party is the trustee, and the lender is the beneficiary.

Federal Housing Administration (FHA)   A branch of the U.S. Department of Housing and Urban Development (HUD); its basic function is to direct housing in a way that Congress mandates by issuing mortgage insurance to institutional lenders on the loans they make. With such loan insurance, lenders are willing to lend with smaller down payments and at lower rates of interest.

Federal National Mortgage Association (FNMA)   One of the largest agencies that buys mortgages from lenders and resells them as securities on the secondary mortgage market.

FHA loan   A low-rate mortgage offered by the Federal Housing Administration (FHA) to buyers who are willing to make a down payment as small as 3 percent.

First mortgage   A mortgage that is in first position and has priority as a lien over all other mortgages.

Flip   To sell a property wholesale to another investor or at retail, usually shortly after purchase.

Foreclosure   A legal procedure in which property used as security for a debt is sold or transferred to satisfy the debt in the event of default in payment of the mortgage note or default of other terms in the mortgage document. Following foreclosure, the title of the property either reverts to the holder of the mortgage or to a third party who may purchase the property at the foreclosure sale; the property then becomes free of all encumbrances subsequent to the mortgage.

Good-faith estimate   An estimate of the costs a borrower will incur, including inspection fees and loan-processing charges.

Grace period   A set number of days during which a debtor may cure a delinquency without penalty.

Grantee   The person to whom the title of a property is granted.

Grantor   A seller who grants title to a buyer.

Hard-money lender   A private investor, individual, or company with cash to lend, usually at higher rates and based on the equity of a property as opposed to the income or credit of a borrower.

Home equity line of credit (HELOC)   A loan secured by property that can be repaid and borrowed again at the property owner's convenience.

Home equity loan   A loan taken out by a homeowner against the equity in his or her home.

HUD 1 settlement statement   A standard form used to itemize services and fees charged to the borrower by the lender or broker. The borrower has the right to inspect the HUD-1 one day prior to or the day of the settlement. The form is filled out by the settlement agent who will conduct the settlement.

Hypothecate   To use something as security and still retain possession of it.

Indemnity   A loss or damage endured by another person that one is fully responsible for.

Joint ownership   Ownership of a property by two or more parties.

Judgment   A final court decision that settles a dispute and determines the rights and obligations of the parties involved.

Judicial foreclosure   A foreclosure process that involves a court action.

Land contract   An agreement transferring property ownership and withholding title transfer until the majority or entire purchase price is received.

Lease   An accord that requires payment of rent to possess real estate for a specified period of time.

Lease option   A lease conveying to the lessee the right to purchase a property for a specified period of time.

Lien   A claim or charge on a property for payment of some debt.

Lis pendens   Legal action pending; after default, a formal notice of default that is filed against the property.

Loss mitigation department   The department of lending company that works with homeowners to avoid foreclosure.

Lot book report   The title record report given by a title company that announces any encumbrances recorded against the property.

Marketable title   A title with no claims or defects that could otherwise hinder a property being sold.

Mechanic's lien   A claim against a property, building, or improvement that secures a priority of payment of the price or value of work performed and materials furnished.

Mortgage   An interest in land created by a written document that is security for repayment of a debt.

Multiple Listings Service (MLS)   A database of property listings from local real estate agents; for-sale-by-owner properties are not included.

Nonpayment   Failure to pay. Typically lenders allow occasional late payments on mortgages for a small fee and a notation on the borrower's credit report. However, after the third month, a lender generally sends a past-due notification of nonpayment.

Notice of default (NOD)   A notice sent out by the lender when a mortgage payment is late in an attempt to cure or make the loan current.

Notice of rescission   A legal document used when the defaulting party has cured or corrected a default.

Notice of sale   The notice of an impending foreclosure sale required by the state. It recites the legal description of the property being foreclosed on and gives the time, date, and place of the pending sale.

Offer to purchase   A contract expressing someone's willingness to purchase a certain property on terms expressed in the offer.

Owner financing (seller financing)   A creative method in real estate where the seller of a property agrees to finance all or some of the property. In a sense, the owner acts like a bank.

Phantom bid   A nonexistent bid acknowledged by the auctioneer to create the illusion of a bid and to encourage other bidders to raise their bids.

Power of sale   A clause commonly inserted in mortgages and deeds of trusts that are in default, giving the mortgagee (or trustee) the right and power to advertise and sell the mortgaged property at public auction to satisfy the debt.

Preforeclosure   A term used to refer to properties with delinquent mortgages and prior to foreclosure auction or sale.

Puffing   A price-enhancing technique that may originate with someone employed by the seller to raise the price on a property with fictitious bids.

Quit title   An action at law to remove an adverse claim or cloud from the title of property.

Quitclaim deed   A deed of conveyance that releases any title, interest, or claim that the grantor may have in the premises.

Real estate owned (REO)   Real estate that has reverted back to a lender or bank after foreclosure and unsuccessful sale attempts.

Recorder   A public official who is responsible for keeping all the records of real estate transactions.

Redemption period   The time allotted to the mortgagor to reclaim his or her property after it has been sold at an auction; not all states allow a redemption period.

Reserve price   The minimum price a seller is willing to accept for a property sold at auction; if a sale is subject to a reserve, it's subject to the seller's approval.

Seller financing   A creative method in a real estate transaction that allows the seller of a property to finance all or some of the property.

Sheriff's sale   Sale of a property to satisfy a debt or judgment.

Shill   An employee of an auction company who bids against legitimate bidders to run up the price.

Short sale   A sale in which a lender agrees to take less in payment for a property than the value of the loan on the property.

Simultaneous closing   A creative approach to financing and flipping properties in which the mortgage created by the seller is sold to the buyer at the closing. It is also called back-to-back closing.

Subject to   A phrase that indicates the transfer of rights to pay a debt from one party to another, with the original party remaining liable for the debt if the second party defaults.

Survey   The process by which a parcel of land is measured and its boundaries and contents set forth.

Tax deed   A type of deed used to convey title after real property is sold at auction by public authority for nonpayment of taxes.

Tax lien   A lien on real estate in favor of a state or local government that may be foreclosed on for the nonpayment of taxes.

Tenant   A person in possession of real property with the owner's permission.

Tenant at sufferance   A person who after rightfully being in possession of a rented premises continues to live in that premises after his right has terminated.

Tenant at will   A person who holds possession of premises with the owner's permission.

Tie bids   Two or more bids in a property auction that come in at the same price and at the same time; usually the auctioneer accepts the one he recognized first as the new highest bidder.

Title   Evidence of ownership of property or land.

Title company   A firm that examines properties to ensure that their titles are clear and free of any encumbrances. Such companies also issue title insurance.

Title insurance   An insurance policy that provides protection for lenders and buyers against any losses caused by defects in the title.

Torrens title   A type of title (named for Sir Robert Richard Torrens) that contains a listing of all legal instruments (mortgages, judgments, liens) that have been recorded on the property from its origin.

Trust account   A special account used by a broker or escrow agent to safeguard funds for a buyer or seller.

Trust deed A three-party security instrument conveying the legal title to real property as security for the repayment of a loan. The owner is called the trustor. The neutral third party to whom the bare legal title is conveyed (and who is called on to liquidate the property if need be) is the trustee. The lender is the beneficiary. When the loan is paid off, the trustee is directed by the beneficiary to issue a deed of reconveyance to the trustor, which extinguishes the trust deed lien.

Trustee's deed A deed given to the successful high bidder after a foreclosure auction.

Trustee's sale An auction during which a trustee may sell a property that has defaulted in an effort to pay the outstanding debt that is owed.

Unsecured debt Debt not secured by collateral.

Upset price The opening bid amount that begins the auction bidding during a foreclosure sale.

Veterans Administration (VA) loan A loan available to veterans that allows the purchase of a house without a down payment.

Warranty deed A deed in which the grantor warrants good, clear title.

Wraparound mortgage A financing technique in which the payment of the existing mortgage is continued by the seller and a new, higher-interest loan, which is larger than the existing mortgage, is paid by the borrower.

Yield The return on investment or the amount of profit stated as a percentage of the amount invested.

Zoning A set of regulations that control the use of land within a jurisdiction.

ABOUT THE AUTHOR

Real estate educator, mentor, and investor Jeff Adams is among the nation's leading experts in foreclosure investing. His automated systems for attracting property buyers, sellers, and private lenders have helped all kinds of people—full- and part-time investors alike—achieve their financial dreams. Adams personally has done hundreds of real estate deals—all while investing only part-time!

Trained as a firefighter and hazardous materials specialist, Adams spent more than 20 years fighting fires in Southern California before turning to real estate full time. "I loved being a firefighter, but I wanted financial independence for my family and I couldn't do that as a firefighter," says Adams. "When I started out as a part-time real estate investor, there were no how-to manuals. I learned 'under fire' what works and what doesn't. Because I had another full-time job, out of necessity I developed processes and procedures to streamline real estate investing. I literally didn't have the time to waste!"

Today Adams has traded battling some of Southern California's deadliest fires to sharing his expertise on the right way to fight—and/or avoid—the more figurative financial fires that can be a part of real estate investing.

When not on the road sharing his real estate expertise at seminars around the country, Adams lives in Southern California with his wife Kristina and twin daughters.

BONUS OFFER JUST FOR YOU!

SPECIAL SCHOLARSHIP TO JEFF ADAMS
FORECLOSURE ACADEMY

Congratulations! With the purchase of my book, *How to Buy Bank-Owned Properties for Pennies on the Dollar: A Guide to REO Investing in Today's Market*, you're a step closer to your financial independence. The next step is yours for free!

As a bonus with this book, I would like to offer you and a guest a scholarship to my Foreclosure Academy exclusive three-day accelerated training event. A ticket to the event sells for $2,997 or more, but it's yours for FREE. That's right—because you bought this book, you and one guest are invited to attend one three-day training event at absolutely no charge. Training events are held regularly at various locations coast to coast, and registration and attendance are subject to availability or schedule changes. Seating is extremely limited.

Register today at www.REOWealthEvent.com to claim your one-time scholarship and secure your place at my next Foreclosure Academy exclusive training event.

The opportunities to cash in on real estate owned (REO) properties are growing bigger and faster than you've ever dreamed. As a reader of my book, you now understand why—from up-and-down home prices to politics, lending practices, economics, and more. Now is your opportunity to cash in. The next step in the process—attendance at my renowned Foreclosure Academy—is FREE, my gift to you for buying this book.

Thousands of people have used my Real Estate Profit Systems to put their real estate investing on steroids. Now you can, too. This is a rare opportunity to learn more about my moneymaking systems at absolutely no risk to you.

WHAT OTHERS ARE SAYING ABOUT JEFF ADAMS FORECLOSURE ACADEMY

Randall Wall (Salt Lake City, Utah): *"I have been incredibly fortunate to have listened to a presentation by Jeff Adams. Using Jeff's products and expertise that he has so generously shared, I have generated at least $100,000 in revenue each year using these products and have brought in many times that in private funds to purchase my properties."*

S. Smith (Paramount, California): *"At the Jeff Adams Foreclosure [Academy] training event ... I actually got hands-on training for buying properties at auction. ... Jeff Adams didn't hold anything back. I learned step-by-step what to do. He is passionate about his real estate investing and I got a chance to experience that passion. ... This was a fantastic event, and now I've got the tools."*

Kit Critchlow (Scottsdale, Arizona): *"I recently attended Jeff Adams's four-day boot camp in Los Angeles. I was not sure what to expect. I was blown away by the information I gathered at the event. It exceeded my expectations by 500 percent. I now have the information I need to make a career in real estate. Being a software engineer, I can also provide an opinion on his web tools. He really has a well-organized, powerful set of web tools for the real estate investor. Jeff's real estate web knowledge is fantastic."*

Chuck Dickson (Glendale, Arizona): *"When I attended Jeff Adams's ... seminar, it was awesome. We did a deal in class right over the phone, and learned a ton of info that I didn't get from many other seminars. It's a definite must if you're going to be in real estate investing."*

Here's a small sample of the invaluable information and training you'll get from my Foreclosure Academy exclusive training event:

- Three days of hard-hitting REO buying and selling tactics—strategies not mentioned in the book and secrets that have helped me and hundreds of other people like you to make millions of dollars. These are tips and tricks no one anywhere else is teaching that force your business to succeed.
- Information-packed sessions of advanced strategies that work now! These are buying and selling real estate tips that you can take with you and that applied right will help you dominate your market.
- High-level networking with potential joint-venture partners who can make your business boom.
- Question-and-answer panels to help troubleshoot your investing and real estate issues.
- The availability of one-on-one personal coaching to accelerate your business and your learning curve.
- An introduction to my turnkey online business model that can put your investing success almost on autopilot.

You've read this book, so I know you're serious about multiplying your income and gaining control over your finances. Now, with the help of my Foreclosure Academy training event, you can learn new and unparalleled tips on how to develop your business so that it nearly runs itself. A huge part of being a successful investor is staying ahead of the competition by attracting the sellers, leveraging all the tools available—including emerging technology—and finding sellers where they are. That's what the next step—my Foreclosure Academy training event—is all about.

Plenty of real estate gurus and products promise you that you'll make a fortune in real estate, yet they fail to deliver. The Jeff Adams Foreclosure Academy delivers and can make the difference for you and your business. It's not about pie-in-the-sky dreams. My associates and I instead deliver cold, hard facts and procedures. We show you exactly what it takes to make your REO buying and selling dreams come true.

So take advantage of this limited-time free offer and register today for your scholarship to the next Jeff Adams Foreclosure Academy exclusive three-day event. Go to www.REOWealthEvent.com, or call my office now, at 1-800-574-9221.

JEFF ADAMS FORECLOSURE ACADEMY SCHOLARSHIP

LIMITED-TIME OFFER: As a bonus with the purchase of Jeff Adams's *How to Buy Bank-Owned Properties for Pennies on the Dollar: A Guide to REO Investing in Today's Market*, you and one guest are entitled to free admission to attend one Jeff Adams Foreclosure Academy live three-day accelerated training event. Training events are offered at various locations, and attendance is subject to availability or schedule changes. This is your once-in-a-lifetime free opportunity to jump-start your REO investing career and realize your dreams of financial independence.

To register today to claim your one-time scholarship and secure your place at Jeff Adams's next Foreclosure Academy accelerated training event, visit www.REOWealthEvent.com or call 1-800-574-9221.

INDEX